HISTORIC KNOXVILLE
AND KNOX COUNTY

CITY CENTER, NEIGHBORHOODS, AND PARKS

A Walking and Touring Guide

A Tag-Along Book
by Russ Manning and
Sondra Jamieson

Bicentennial Edition

Laurel Place
Norris, Tenn.

Printed in the United States of America.

ISBN: 0-9625122-3-0

Front Cover: Knoxville

Published by

        Laurel Place
        P.O. Box 3001
        Norris, TN 37828

Contents

Knox County

Surrounding Areas

Acknowledgments

We are grateful to the Office of the Bicentennial for their encouragement and support during the preparation of this book: Director Sue Clancy, Assistant Director Carolyn Jensen, and Assistants Bobbye Dyslin, Emily Mackebee, Susan Thayer, and Roseanne Wolf. We also thank the Historical Committee of the Bicentennial for their interest and assistance.

Many people gave their time to supply information about their neighborhoods and to show us around: Bob Whetsel of the 4th and Gill Neighborhood; Tim Northcutt, Jean Hall Allen, and Allen Coggins of Old North Knoxville; Knox County Commissioner Mary Lou Horner of Fountain City; Bill Powell of Mechanicsville; Beck Center Executive Director Bob Booker for East Knoxville; Brodie and Grace Baynes and Emmaretta Hough of Island Home; Renelle Bush for Westwood; and Ruth Brown for Westmoreland. Mary Wine, Public Relations Assistant in the UT Office of University Relations, supplied information on the University of Tennessee, and Dr. Milton Klein, University Historian, reviewed the university section. David Harkness supplied information on Old Gray Cemetery.

We thank those who reviewed the manuscript: Ann Bennett, Planner for the Metropolitan Planning Commission; Linda Billman, producer of WBIR-TV's Heartland Series; Steve Cotham, Head of the McClung Historical Collection; David J. Harkness, local historian, retired from UT; Bill Landry of WBIR-TV's The Heartland Series; Virginia Niceley, Knox County Historian; Walter Pulliam, past president of the East Tennessee Historical Society and Chairman of the Historical Committee of the Bicentennial; and staff members of the Office of the Bicentennial.

We also thank the Metropolitan Planning Commission for supplying basic maps from which most of our maps are drawn.

Much of the information in this book is based on the historic sites survey and the historic tours prepared by the Knoxville/Knox County Historic Zoning Commission of the Metropolitan Planning Commission and by Knoxville Heritage, Inc., and the historical references prepared by the East Tennessee Historical Society.

Bicentennial Events

(watch for other events during the year)

December 31, 1990   **Bicentennial Countdown**. A city-wide celebration to launch the activities for the Bicentennial year.

April 12-28, 1991   **Dogwood Arts Festival**. The annual festival of concerts and performances, including Bicentennial historic trolley tours from Market Square and a Bicentennial Children's Parade.

April 21, 1991   **Bicentennial Religious Heritage Celebration**. Displays and a program at Thompson-Boling Arena.

May 24-27, 1991   **Festival on the River**. A gathering on the riverfront.

June 1, 1991   **Statehood Celebration**. An event held at Blount Mansion.

Sept. 6-14, 1991   **Tennessee Valley Fair**. Annual fair held at Chilhowee Park.

October 3-6, 1991   **Knoxville's 200th Birthday Celebration**. A weekend celebration of waterfront activities, fireworks, and festivities.

October 5, 1991   **Bicentennial '91 Parade**. A downtown parade of floats, bands, and clowns.

December 31, 1991   **Bicentennial Finale**. Events held downtown and at the World's Fair Park.

A Bicentennial Welcome

During the 200 years of Knoxville's existence, the city has grown from a frontier outpost to one of the major metropolitan areas in the Southeast. Today's Knoxville is a city of historic buildings and neighborhoods, revitalized business districts and new commercial centers, active university and college campuses, and quality theaters and restaurants.

Beginning Fall 1990, we will be celebrating our city's Bicentennial, calling attention to the rich history of Knoxville and our potential for growth and renewal. The celebration will include many official events of the city and civic groups. But I hope it will also include spontaneous gatherings of Knoxville's citizens to celebrate their individual heritage and the preservation of their culture.

It is fortunate that this Bicentennial celebration coincides with an effort on the part of many in our city to revitalize our downtown area and to restore the prestige of our neighborhoods. You will see the results of this work on your visit to Knoxville during this period of celebration. The City is grateful to these business, civic, and neighborhood leaders who have done much to return Knoxville to a place of culture and beauty. I encourage them to continue and commit the City's support.

But Knoxville is also grateful to the individual citizens of our city who have accomplished much on a small scale. Those who have lovingly restored an historic home in one of our older neighborhoods. Those who have faithfully maintained a community garden or park. Those who have raised their voices when an historic structure was threatened. And all of those who have chosen to live and do business in our city.

There is much to see and do in Knoxville, in both heritage and culture. I hope you will walk the streets of our city center, visit our neighborhoods and parks, and tour the surrounding county to learn of our history and meet our people. Join with us in celebrating Knoxville's 200th birthday.

Victor Ashe
Mayor

The Need for Preservation

As you enjoy the history represented in the buildings and homes discussed in this book, imagine what it must have been like to build a log house on the frontier, as did James White, Nicholas Gibbs, and John Adair. Or pretend you're sitting on a wide, cool front porch on a summer evening, visiting with neighbors in Fort Sanders, Park City, Old North Knoxville, or 4th and Gill. Or watch for the farm wagons bringing produce to sell at Market Square. Or listen for the sound of train whistles and the cries of street vendors in the warehouse district along Jackson, Gay, and Central when the train was Knoxville's link with the outside world.

In this year of Knoxville's Bicentennial, it is particularly appropriate that this collection of walking and driving tours has been published. As you follow the tours, you will find many illustrations of our early history. The buildings and place names of Knoxville and Knox County provide a vivid illustration of the events and people that shaped this area.

This book is possible because many historic resources have survived. Many of our early buildings have been rehabilitated and restored. They speak clearly of the lifestyles and architecture of the era in which they were built and the dedication of their present owners to that history.

Still, there are many resources which are threatened. If we are to continue to appreciate the history represented in buildings, it is important that we try not to lose another. Means must be used to preserve our historic buildings. There are tax incentives for income-producing rehabilitation projects; there are houses that offer the tradition of fine architecture and close proximity to the work place; there are legal methods to protect facades of historic buildings and encourage their preservation.

Preservation is born of sensitivity and enthusiasm. It is the hope of the Knoxville Historic Zoning Commission that this volume will foster that spirit.

Art Clancy, Chairman
Knoxville Historic Zoning Commission

Knoxville

3

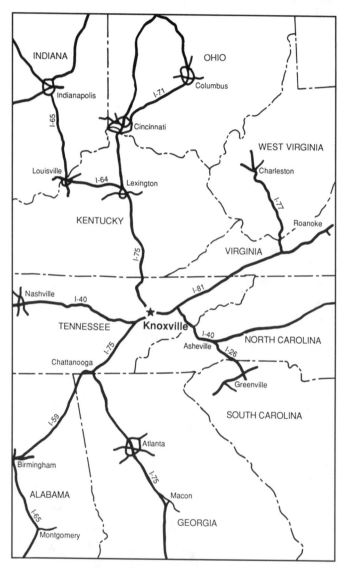

Getting There: In addition to I-40 and I-75 intersecting in Knoxville, the city is served by commercial airlines at McGhee Tyson Airport 9 miles south of the city and by Greyhound-Trailways Bus Lines with a station on Magnolia Avenue.

Geography

Knoxville lies in the Great Valley of East Tennessee, with the Unaka Mountains on the east and the Cumberland Plateau on the west. The fifty-mile-wide valley consists of so many low mountain ridges and shallow valleys that it is also called the "Valley and Ridge Province." The ridges and valleys run parallel, northeast to southwest, due to continental forces that rippled the face of the land about 250 million years ago and subsequent erosion that dipped out troughs between hard-rock ridges.

In 1785, James White came to the Knoxville region with his family to settle in the forks of the river where the Holston and French Broad Rivers meet to create the Tennessee River. The Tennessee was then called the "Holston River" as far south as the Little Tennessee River. The name came from Stephen Holston, a pioneer from Virginia who explored the river system in 1748. The section of the Holston River below the confluence with the French Broad became known as the "Tennessee River" in the late 1800s, a name appropriated from the Little Tennessee which once flowed past the Cherokee town of Tanassee. The French Broad derives its name from the proximity of the Broad River to the French Broad's headwaters in North Carolina. The Broad River flows east to the Atlantic, while the French Broad flows west toward what was then a French region of the Mississippi River Valley.

In 1786, James White relocated a few miles west of the confluence of the two rivers to a hill overlooking the Tennessee River, then the Holston. His property was bounded on the east by First Creek, at first called "White's Creek," and on the west by Second Creek, so named because they were the first and second creeks below the joining of the Holston and French Broad Rivers.

The community that grew up around James White's fort became the City of Knoxville, which expanded in all directions and for a time was the capital of the State of Tennessee. Today, Knoxville, Tennessee, is situated near the geographic center of the eastern United States. It is the commercial center of a large metropolitan area and the county seat of Knox County.

A Brief History

A succession of native American peoples were the first to frequent the area that became East Tennessee. By the time white men appeared, the Cherokees dominated the region. While they claimed the land that would become Knox County, the Cherokees' major towns were along the Little Tennessee River 40 miles south of present-day Knoxville.

The first white settlers in East Tennessee were of Scotch-Irish descent and came from Virginia and North and South Carolina. James White, the first known settler at Knoxville, was from Rowan County, later Iredell County, North Carolina. It was at White's Fort that William Blount, Governor of the Southwest Territory, negotiated the Treaty of Holston with the Cherokees in 1791, which opened up what is now Knox County to settlement.

In the same year, White sold land around his fort for the establishment of a town that Blount named "Knoxville." Lots were sold at lottery on October 3, 1791. Knox County was established the following year, June 11, 1792. Knoxville served as the capital of the Territory and, when the State of Tennessee was formed in 1796, as the capital of the state, which it remained most of the time through 1817. The City of Knoxville was incorporated in 1815.

The first train arrived in Knoxville in 1855, and the presence of the railroad placed the city in a strategic position during the Civil War. The Confederates first occupied Knoxville and the East Tennessee region. Then in the summer of 1863, Major General Ambrose E. Burnside and his Union troops invaded. The Confederates in Knoxville were called south to support the conflict at Chattanooga, and so Burnside's forces swept into the unoccupied city and took control. In the fall of 1863, Lieutenant-General James Longstreet and his Confederate troops tried to retake Knoxville, but their effort failed, and the city saw little action for the remainder of the war.

Because of its railroads, Knoxville after the Civil War eventually became the central location for shipping East Tennessee products throughout the Southeast. Besides agriculture, other industries were established in the area because of the accessibility of natural resources and the rail lines. In the period 1880-87, 97 factories were built—iron mills, machine shops, cloth mills, apparel factories, furniture factories, and marble quarries and finishing plants. Fortunes were made, and many office buildings, warehouses, and mansions were built.

As the population grew, especially with the freed slaves and Appalachian whites that came to Knoxville looking for jobs in the fast growing economy, the city expanded. Local developers and architects built houses and subdivisions away from the city center for the more wealthy, and thus more mobile, people of the city. The city center became increasingly a commercial area with residential areas spreading beyond the city limits, even as the limits were expanded to include many of these neighborhoods.

The industrialization of Knoxville continued until the Great Depression in the 1930s. After which, Knoxville suffered a gradual decline in its industries and a deterioration of housing in the city center that resulted in an increase in the move of the more advantaged to the suburbs, with businesses following.

Several attempts in the 1960s to reinvigorate the city center as a retail center were only temporarily successful. The trend for shopping to be done in outlying malls overcame all efforts. Then in the 1970s, new city leaders brought a vision of the city as a business and financial district. They conceived the idea of an energy exposition as the focus for revitalization. The exposition grew beyond its conception and became the 1982 World's Fair.

In the years since the fair, many business and civic leaders have contributed to the revitalization of Knoxville's city center. New commercial buildings have taken their place beside historic structures restored to their former nobility. City streets are being reworked to recreate the historical atmosphere. Old sections of the city once again have become the mix of residences and commercial establishments they had been in the past. Vacant buildings show that much remains to be done. But in its Bicentennial year, Knoxville is reemerging as one of the major business and financial centers of the Southeast.

Just as Knoxville completes its year of celebration in 1991, Knox County will be embarking on its Bicentennial celebration in 1992.

Walking and Touring

The outings we describe in this guide range from short walks to tours of many miles that we expect you to do by car. These are designated by the words "walk" and "tour." We encourage you to walk whenever indicated because you can take your time and see so much more. But if you wish, the walks may also be done by car, although with a little difficulty. Occasionally the walks go through parks or malls and over pedestrian bridges, and occasionally we direct the walk the wrong way down a one-way street to take you by an important historic site. So if you are touring by car on what is described as a walk and find yourself directed against the flow on a one way street or facing a pedestrian walkway, drive around the block and you should be able to pick up the tour again.

When you do intend to walk, you'll likely drive to the starting place and park. For walks in the city center, there are numerous fee parking lots and spaces on the street with parking meters; so you should be able to find a parking space relatively near the beginning of any tour in the city. For the neighborhood walks, you must search for a nearby parking area or a parking space on the street; you should be able to find a place that does not add much of a walk to get to your starting point.

The walk and tour numbers in the book correspond to the numbers on some of the accompanying maps. These maps are designed only to show you the route to take; you'll probably also need to carry along a map of the entire city to orient yourself and locate the start of the walk or tour.

Each walk or tour in the book is connected to other tours so you may extend your outing to include one or more tours. We list these connections at the beginning of each tour description.

Please respect private property on your outings. Do all your viewing from the public streets and sidewalks. When you are in the neighborhoods or in the county, do not walk into yards or drive into private driveways, even if that means you will not get a good look at a house or building.

As you travel around some of the neighborhoods, you'll sometimes notice pink or white marks in the road. These designate the trail routes for Knoxville's Annual Spring Dogwood Arts Festival. Sometimes our tours follow these dogwood trails, sometimes not. Don't lose your way by following these trails, thinking they mark the route of the walks and tours in this book.

The best times to walk or tour Knoxville are early evenings, when the business traffic has lessened, and weekends, especially Sundays, when the volume of traffic is reduced. If you are out for a walk, you should wear comfortable shoes, preferably walking shoes that are designed to give sure footing and support ankles. You might also want to wear a hat if its a sunny day or take along an umbrella or rain coat if it looks like rain. If you are driving, don't forget to watch the road while you're watching for historic structures.

Although Knoxville is relatively free of street crime compared with other urban areas in the country, you should take normal precautions for a city environment. It is always best to walk with someone else. Don't leave purses and cameras sitting around or loosely held in your hand. If anyone approaches you that you do not wish to speak to, walk away and go on about your business; you'll probably not be followed.

Late evenings can make for some very pleasant walking around the city. But don't walk alone at night, and avoid dark, deserted streets and alleys. There is no point in going into neighborhoods and parks at night, since you'll be able to see very little, except on occasions like lighted tennis and ball games at Tyson Park or lighted driving trails during the Spring Dogwood Arts Festival.

We cannot mention every precaution you should take while following one of our walks or driving tours; so we expect you to take responsibility for your own safety. But don't let this talk of safety discourage you from walking Knoxville. With only a little effort, you can safely and comfortably experience the history and the culture of the city and its neighborhoods.

Whenever we state that a structure is recommended or eligible for listing on the National Register of Historic Places, we are referring to the sites determined as eligible for National Register listing in the Historic Sites Survey and Cultural Resources Plan for Knoxville and Knox County that was completed by the Knoxville/Knox County Historic Zoning Commission.

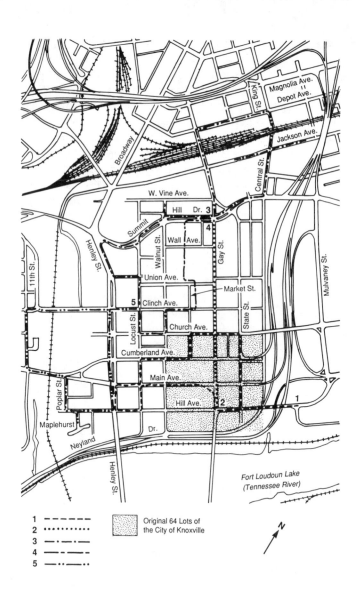

1	– – – – –	
2	• • • • • • • •	Original 64 Lots of
3	– · – · –	the City of Knoxville
4	– · · – · · –	
5	– · · – · ·	

City Center

10

1 The Early Days Walk

1.5 miles
Connections: Gay Street Walk, East Knox County Tour

Attractions: This loop walk through the south end of the city center takes you by the oldest buildings in the city, including the first known structure in Knoxville.

Start: Begin at James White's Fort located at 205 E. Hill Avenue. If you are just entering the city, take the Business Loop off I-40 and then get off at the 441S/Smoky Mtns./Cumberland Ave. exit. At State Street, turn right, and then right again at Church Avenue, which crosses back over the Business Loop. Turn right on Mulvaney Street. You'll pass the Civic Auditorium and Coliseum on the left with the Hyatt Regency on the hill. When Mulvaney joins Hill Avenue, keep straight and curve around to the right, where you'll find the James White Fort on the right.

Description: James White with his wife, Mary Lawson, and their children came from North Carolina in 1785 to the region that would later become Tennessee. White had explored the area earlier with James Conner, F. A. Ramsey, and others. The men returned later with their families to settle in the region.

White was entitled to a land grant from the State of North Carolina for his service as captain in the North Carolina militia during the Revolutionary War. Instead of accepting that claim, he purchased in accordance with North Carolina's Land Act of 1783 other lands between the Holston and French Broad Rivers, settling there first, and between First and Second Creeks on the north bank of the Tennessee River. With his neighbor, James Conner, White moved to this second tract of land in 1786, one thousand acres that would later become the City of Knoxville. He erected a cabin on a hill near where First Creek joins the Tennessee River.

White's cabin became a first stop for other settlers moving into the region. To accommodate these guests and to protect them

James White's Fort

and his own family from belligerent Cherokees who did not like their lands appropriated, White built three smaller cabins that, with his own, formed the four corners of a stockade of upright poles. The structure became known as **James White's Fort**.

The fort originally stood on what is now the east side of State Street between Clinch and Union Avenues. When business development threatened to destroy the main cabin, which was all that remained, it was bought and moved in 1906 by Isaiah Ford. In 1960, the City Association of Women's Clubs purchased the house and moved it to its present location on Hill Avenue.

Since then, other log structures have been donated to the project and James White's Fort has been reconstructed with White's house anchoring the structure in history. With an admission fee, you can take a guided tour of the fort, where you'll see White's original cherry table, study desk, wine cabinet, several of his tools, and part of a tub mill.

From James White's Fort, walk west on Hill Avenue toward Gay Street. You'll cross over the **Hill Avenue Bridge**, built in 1936 to span the First Creek Valley. The bridge now passes over part of the Business Loop with First Creek flowing through a subterranean passage. Long range plans for city revitalization call for resurrecting First Creek.

Just before Gay Street, you'll find the **Blount Mansion** complex on the south side of the street at 200 W. Hill Avenue.

In 1790, William Blount, who had been a representative in the North Carolina state legislature and a delegate of the state to the Constitutional Convention and a signer of the U.S. Constitution, was appointed by Pres. George Washington to be governor of the Territory South of the River Ohio. The territory had been created by the federal government out of the western lands given up by the State of North Carolina. Blount first headquartered at a home in upper east Tennessee, called "Rocky Mount," but soon decided that the capital for the new "Southwest Territory," as it was called, should be located near the confluence of the French Broad and Holston Rivers.

Blount moved to James White's Fort in 1791 where he negotiated the Treaty of Holston with 41 Cherokee chiefs. The treaty established a new southern boundary between the United States and the Cherokee Nation that opened up the region around

Blount Mansion (David Cann)

James White's Fort to settlement, supposedly without harassment from the Indians. With land purchased from White, Blount established the capitol of the Southwest Territory at that location and called it "Knoxville" for his superior at the time, Henry Knox, U.S. Secretary of War and head of Indian affairs.

The site for the new city was surveyed by Charles McClung, the son-in-law of James White. Streets were laid out, many ending up with names from streets in Philadelphia where McClung was from—Walnut, Market, Church, and Broad—and Baltimore—Gay Street. The blocks defined by the streets were subdivided into 64 half-acre lots. With the selling of these lots by public lottery on October 3, 1791, Knoxville was considered founded as a town.

To help his wife and family adjust to life on the frontier, Blount built a two-story house that, because it was one of the first frame houses west of the mountains, was called "Bount's Mansion." Furnished in period furniture, the house is today open to the public with an admission fee. Behind the mansion, you'll find a detached kitchen, gardens, and Governor Blount's Office. Blount was a promoter of statehood for the territory, and it is thought that Blount wrote the Tennessee Constitution in his office. When the state was established, Blount became one of the first two senators from Tennessee to the U.S. Congress. Because of the historical importance of this site, Blount Mansion is designated a National Historic Landmark, the only such designation in Knoxville.

The visitor center for the Blount Mansion is the **Craighead-Jackson House** built in 1818 by John Craighead and now on the National Register of Historic Places. Dr. George Jackson bought the home in the mid-1850s and lived there until the late 1870s. An upstairs museum in the house tells of the preservation efforts for both the Craighead-Jackson House and Blount Mansion.

From the Blount Mansion complex, walk north up State Street, which is across Hill Avenue from the Craighead-Jackson House. In three blocks, you'll come to the **First Presbyterian Church** on the northeast corner of State Street and Church Avenue at 620 State Street. This land was originally James White's turnip patch, and his fort stood just north of here. White donated the land for the church and the adjacent cemetery in

1792. The church was organized by the Rev. Samuel Carrick. The present Neoclassical building was erected around 1902.

Many of the early founders of the city are buried in the cemetery next to the church. The gravestones are numbered. Samuel Carrick, who was also the first President of Blount College that later became the University of Tennessee, is buried at #2 gravesite. John Craighead is at #11; William and Mary Blount, #26 and #27; and James White, #35.

Across from the church and cemetery, notice **The Glencoe**, an apartment building erected about 1900.

From the First Presbyterian Church, walk west on Church Street. In the one block before Gay Street, you'll pass on the left the **Knoxville News-Sentinel and Knoxville Journal** building that houses the operations of the two daily papers. The *News-Sentinel* was founded in 1886; the *Journal*, which began in 1885, descended from the *Knoxville Whig* that had published since the early part of the century. On the right, you'll see the **Elliott Apt. Hotel** built about 1900. The **Knoxville Business College Building** at 209 Church Avenue was built about 1916 as an office and apartment building; it became the business college in 1944, which is now located on N. 5th Avenue. Notice the Romanesque entryway. The abandoned college building, which is on the National Register, and the Elliott and the Glencoe are contributing structures to the Gay Street Commercial Historic District.

Continue west on Church, and cross Gay Street. You'll pass on the right **One** and **Two Centre Square**, some of the newest office buildings in the city. You'll notice in the corner plaza a bronze sculpture of a man in a row boat. The theme of the sculpture by David Phelps of California is optimism and perseverance under adverse circumstances.

At the northwest corner of Market Street, you'll see the **Bank of Knoxville Building**, which was designed by the architectural firm of Barber & McMurry and constructed in 1926 with Renaissance Revival detailing. It was originally called the "General Building." Charles Barber was the son of the nationally known residence architect George F. Barber, who had his base in Knoxville. Charles at first joined his father's firm but later formed a partnership with Ben McMurry. Barber & McMurry designed many Knoxville houses built in the 1920s and '30s.

16

They also designed commercial and public buildings, including Church Street United Methodist Church and the YMCA and YWCA in the city center and Hoskins Library on the University of Tennessee Campus. The Barber & McMurry firm still operates in Knoxville but no longer has a Barber as part of the company.

On the southwest corner of Church and Market, you'll find the **Cherokee**, which now contains optometrists' offices and a bookstore. The Cherokee and the Bank of Knoxville buildings, along with others south on Market and west on Church, have been proposed to constitute a Church-Market Historic District that includes buildings constructed in 1900-1925 in the Victorian Vernacular and Renaissance Revival styles. This district represents the combination of commercial and residential space that was common in the city in the early part of the century. West on Church, you'll find architect offices in **The Ely** building at 406 W. Church that was originally a medical office built about 1916. And then at 414 W. Church stands a Volunteers of America emergency shelter that until the early 1970s was **Mann's Mortuary**; notice "MANN" in stained glass on the second floor. The building, constructed about 1915, was designed by R. F. Graf and Sons, an architectural firm that also designed many structures in Knoxville. At the corner of Market and Church, turn south on Market; you'll see other buildings on the right to be included in the proposed historic district—**The Cunningham**, **The Stuart**, and **The Cate**, built about 1900.

Directly ahead at the end of Market, you'll see the **Whittle Communications Corporate Headquarters** under construction. The campus-like structure will be completed in 1991 and will house Whittle Communications, L. P., a nationally known media company that produces a variety of magazines, information centers, and Channel 1 TV for school classrooms.

When you get to Cumberland Avenue, turn right. At the end of the block, you'll find **St. John's Episcopal Cathedral** at 413 W. Cumberland Avenue. The church was organized in 1844; J. W. Yost designed the present structure, which was built in 1892 in the Richardsonian Romanesque style with Gothic detailing. The section on the right was added in the 1980s.

Directly across the street, you'll see the **Sevier-Park House** at 422 W. Cumberland Avenue, one of the oldest structures remaining in Knoxville. John Sevier laid the foundation of the house in 1797. Sevier was one of the leaders of the Overmountain Men in the Battle of Kings Mountain during the Revolutionary War. He was later governor of the State of Franklin, a self-declared state within North Carolina's western lands that became part of the Southwest Territory when it was formed in 1790 and finally part of the State of Tennessee in 1796. Sevier became Tennessee's first governor.

While trying to build his house in Knoxville, Sevier ran out of money after forming the basement and raising the foundation only three feet. So instead he rented a house in the city from Charles McClung; Sevier and his family also spent much time at Marble Springs, their country home about six miles south of Knoxville. Sevier sold the Knoxville property to James Dunlap in 1807, who sold it to James Park in 1812, who then finished the construction. You can still see the change in bricks about three feet up from the ground where the change in construction took place. Park and then his son, Dr. James Park, Jr., lived in the house. Park, a merchant and trustee of East Tennessee College (later the University of Tennessee), was twice the mayor of Knoxville, 1818-1821 and 1824-1826; his son was a Presbyterian minister and was for a time principal of the Tennessee School for the Deaf in Knoxville, and later, pastor of the First Presbyterian Church.

Today, the Sevier-Park House is the headquarters for the Knoxville Academy of Medicine and is on the National Register. The building has been modified. The entrance was once on the east side of the house, and a wing was added on the back in 1968. The house has been revitalized to its present state with the help of Gene Burr, an architect and planner specializing in historic preservation and planning. Burr also helped in the restoration of the old Knox County Courthouse that you'll see later on this walk.

Cross Walnut Street and continue west one more block on Cumberland Avenue to Locust Street. On the northeast corner of Locust and Cumberland stands the **John J. Duncan Federal Building**, a new construction named for the long-time U.S. congressman and former mayor of Knoxville. On the northwest corner is the **Tennessee Supreme Court and Court of Appeals**, designed by Baumann and Baumann, a family architect firm that designed much of the architecture in Knoxville. The firm was begun by Joseph F. Baumann in the 1870s and became Baumann Brothers in the 1880s when Albert B. Baumann joined the firm. When Albert B., Jr., joined the company, it became Baumann and Baumann. The Baumann firms designed many residences and commercial and public buildings in the city.

Turn left on Locust. On your right for nearly the full length of the block is the **Medical Arts Building**, designed by Manley and Young of Lexington and built in 1929-30 to house physician offices. The building, now on the National Register, faces Main Avenue at 603 Main. A recent rehabilitation has brought the building back to a nearly original condition. The building is Gothic style with ornamental buttresses and with Tudor arches over the garage entrance and main doors. The facade is probably the best example of terra cotta in the city. Still used for offices, the building also has shops and a restaurant on the street level. On your left along this block is the U. S. Post Office, which you'll reach again later in the walk.

At Main Avenue, turn right in front of the Medical Arts Building. On the left is the **Main Place Office Building**, a renovation that contains multi-use office space. At the end of the block, turn left on Henley Street. Across Henley, you'll see the **Church Street United Methodist Church**, which is included in the World's Fair Park Walk. At the corner of Hill Avenue, notice **Henley Street Bridge** over the Tennessee River, which is also called "Fort Loudoun Lake" because the river is backed up all the way to Knoxville from the Tennessee Valley Authority's Fort Loudoun Dam to the south near Lenoir City, Tennessee. The bridge was constructed in 1930 with six concrete arch spans. The street and the bridge are named for Col. David Henley, who was the Southwest Territory agent and superintendent of Indian Affairs for the U.S. War Department, 1793-1801; it was in Henley's office at the southwest corner of Gay and Church that the state's first constitutional convention was held in 1796.

Turn left on Hill Avenue. The first block on Hill Avenue had been proposed as a **Hill Avenue Historic District** that consisted of a collection of residential buildings constructed in 1885-1925. Some of these have since been torn down for a parking lot. Four of the structures remain. On the north corner of Hill and Henley stands an apartment building constructed as a residence about 1910. Also on the left, you'll see the **Lord Lindsey**, a Neoclassical residence built about 1900 by A. P. Lockett; it was purchased by the First Church of Christ, Scientist and remodeled into a church in 1927; it has now been renovated into a discotheque. Across the street is a building that houses law offices and next to it an apartment building called "**The River House**" that was built for apartments about 1925 and recently renovated.

At Locust Avenue, turn left one block to Main Avenue and turn right. You'll be walking in front of the **Sovran Bank**, a new construction. Across Main Avenue, you'll see the **U.S. Post Office** at 501 Main. Completed in early 1934 and used also for federal offices and courts, the post office is on the National Register. The style is Modern and Art Deco, and the construction is of East Tennessee marble. The walks in front of the building are marble and also Crab Orchard sandstone from the Cumberland Plateau to the west. The eagles at the top of the building were carved by an Italian immigrant who worked for a Knoxville marble business, John J. Craig and Company. The building was designed by the Baumann and Baumann architect firm.

Adjacent to the Sovran Bank, you'll find the **First Baptist Church** at 510 Main Avenue. The church was designed by Dougherty and Gardner of Nashville and built in 1923 in the Neoclassical style.

Continue east on Main Avenue and cross Walnut Street. On your left will be the front of the Whittle Communications Headquarters, and to the right you'll see the modern **City-County Building** set back with a small park in front. Just past the walkway entrance to the City-County Building, you'll come to the old **Knox County Courthouse** on your right on the corner of Main and Gay Street. A mix of Colonial Revival, Romanesque, and Eastlake styles, the National Register courthouse was designed by Palliser & Palliser of New York and built by Stephenson & Getaz in 1885 on the site of the first blockhouse in the area; federal troops were garrisoned here after Knoxville became the capital of the Southwest Territory. Additions on both sides of the building were constructed in 1920-21. The entire building was restored in 1989 and still houses county offices.

Old Knox County Courthouse

The arched gateway to the courthouse grounds on the corner of Main and Gay is dedicated to Dr. John Mason Boyd, a physician in the 1800s. Markers and a statue on the grounds commemorate the service of veterans and also Knoxville's place in history as the territorial capital and as the state capital. In addition, John Sevier and his second wife, Catherine Sherrill, are interred here. Sevier died of a fever in 1815 while surveying the boundary of Creek lands added to the U.S. He was buried near Fort Decatur, Alabama, but was reinterred here in 1889. Catherine, who in her later years had moved to Russellville, Alabama, died and was buried there but was reinterred on the courthouse grounds in 1922. The original tombstones of Sevier and Catherine Sherrill, known as "Bonny Kate," are in the wall of the northeast corner of the courthouse.

There is also a marker on the grounds for Sevier's first wife, Sarah Hawkins, who died in 1780 during an Indian uprising, which perhaps partially explains Sevier's later antagonism toward the Indians. In over thirty battles that Sevier fought with the native Americans, he earned the epithet "Scourge of the Cherokees."

Turn south on Gay Street along the east side of the courthouse to Hill Avenue. At the northeast corner of Hill and Gay, you'll find the **Andrew Johnson Hotel** at 912 Gay Street, originally the "Tennessee Terrace." Several homes were razed for the construction between 1926 and 1929. The building, designed in the Second Renaissance Revival style by Baumann and Baumann, is on the National Register. The hotel was the tallest building in the city until 1979. It now houses offices and soon **Checkers Restaurant** in the attached solarium.

At this southern end of Gay Street, notice the **Gay Street Bridge** that spans the Tennessee River. Built in 1897, the bridge is a seven-span cantilever truss construction.

From the Andrew Johnson Hotel, you can continue to tour the city by taking the Gay Street Walk north. Or you can return to your starting point by walking east on Hill past the Blount Mansion and back to James White's Fort. From there, you can connect with the East Knox County Tour on Riverside Drive across Hill Avenue from the fort.

2 Gay Street Walk

0.5 mile one way
Connections: Southern Terminal and Warehouse District
Walk, Market Square Walk

Attractions: This walk takes you through the heart of the city center into the Gay Street Commercial Historic District.

Start: Begin at the southern end of Gay Street where The Early Days Walk ends.

Description: From the old **Knox County Courthouse** and the **Andrew Johnson Hotel** at the southern end of Gay Street, walk north on Gay.

Adjacent to the Andrew Johnson stands **Riverview Tower** and then, after you cross Main Avenue, another office building, the **Plaza Tower**. These two tall glass office buildings were originally the headquarters of the Butcher banking empire. Jake Butcher twice unsuccessfully ran for governor of the state and was a major backer of Knoxville's 1982 World's Fair. Butcher had taken over the long-established Hamilton National Bank and renamed it "United American." Butcher and his brother, C. H., who ran the City and County Bank System, garnered national attention when their banking systems collapsed amid charges of fraud and federal banking violations that eventually put both in federal prison. Riverview Tower was to have been the headquarters of C. H. Butcher's bank. Plaza Tower was Jake Butcher's United American Plaza.

The Plaza Tower sits on the site of the Staub Theater that was built for Peter Staub, who opened the theater in 1872. Staub was a Swiss immigrant who later became mayor of Knoxville in 1874-75 and 1881-82 and eventually the U. S. Consul to Switzerland. In the early 1900s the theater became Loew's Theater and then the Lyric. The old three-story building was razed for a parking lot in 1956. **The Lunch Box** on the right of the Plaza

Tower is one of the many places in the city center where you can have lunch.

After crossing Main Avenue, you'll see on the west side of Gay Street the side of the **Whittle Communications Corporate Headquarters**. At the far end of the block, you'll find the **Lamar House-Bijou Theater** at 803 Gay Street. Whittle Communications has taken care to build around the Lamar House on its northeast corner and the Park House on its northwest corner.

The Lamar House was built around 1816 as a residence for Thomas Humes and is attributed to the noted builder Thomas Hope. The house may have never been used as a residence since Humes died about the time it was completed. It became the Knoxville Hotel under the management of Captain Joseph Jackson. It later was known as Jackson's Hotel and then as Pickett's City Hotel. In 1847 when Gay Street was regraded, the section in front of the hotel was lowered about twelve feet, exposing the basement, which became the first floor. The main entrance, which was then on the second floor became a balcony from which over the years many political speeches were made to crowds in the street below. During the 1850s, the building became the Coleman House where large parties and balls were held. In 1856, Sampson and Sterling Lanier became the managers and changed the name to Lamar House. These two men were the grandfather and great uncle of Sidney Lanier, the Georgia poet who extolled the virtues of the South in his work. The Lamar House Hotel was occupied by the military during the Civil War.

The Bijou Theater addition was begun in 1908 and the Lamar House section was renovated. The theater opened in 1909. In later years it served as a movie theater. The purchase and restoration of the building was the first project of Knoxville Heritage, Inc., a community organization formed to help preserve the historic resources of the city and county. One of the restoration architects for the Lamar House was Ron Childress, a founding member and past president of Knoxville Heritage who contributed much time and effort to preservation efforts in the city. Childress's contribution is now remembered in the Ronald E. Childress Memorial Award presented each year by Knoxville Heritage to an individual or organization that has made a special effort in preservation.

24

Lamar House-Bijou Theater

Today, the Lamar House-Bijou Theater has reassumed its place as a cultural focal point for the city center. Knoxville Heritage maintains its offices in the Lamar House section of the building, and **The Bistro**, a restaurant, is located on the left of the theater entrance.

Continue walking north, you'll cross Cumberland Avenue and in one more block Church Avenue where you'll see on the west side of Gay Street the **Two Centre Square** office building that is included in The Early Days Walk. From this point north, you'll walk into the **Gay Street Commercial District**, a National Register historic district encompassing the retail and financial center of the old city. The buildings along the street were once department stores, banks, and pharmacies; there were also hotels, theaters, offices, and residences. The historic district includes 5 buildings listed separately on the National Register and over 30 other structures on Gay and State Streets, Church Avenue, and Summit Hill Drive that contribute to the district. The construction dates of these buildings range from the 1870s through the 1930s.

Gay Street has recently been renovated, a project spearheaded by community organizations, Main Street, Inc., and The DownTown Organization. The renovation was designed to return the look of Gay Street to its heyday. Lighting similar to what was there in earlier days was erected, along with new unobtrusive traffic lights and street benches with no advertising. The old sidewalks were replaced with brick. As you walk along, you'll see some of the bricks have the names of donors engraved in them, the result of a fund-raising project held in 1988-89.

At the northeast corner of Church and Gay, you'll see the **Knoxville Utilities Board** at 626 S. Gay. Then two buildings north stands the **Arcade Building** at 618 S. Gay, a contributing structure to the historic district, designed by R. F. Graf and Sons and built about 1924; until 1958 it housed the *Knoxville Journal*. The adjacent building at 612 S. Gay is the **Mechanics Bank and Trust Company**. Constructed in 1870 and remodeled with an addition in 1923, the Mechanics building is of the Second Renaissance style and is listed on the National Register. It now is an office building and the meeting place of the private Old City Club.

26

At the end of the block, you'll find the **Burwell Building** at 600 S. Gay Street, built in 1908 on the original 1794 site of Blount College. A 1928 addition contains the **Tennessee Theater**, designed by Graven & Magyer of Chicago. The Tennessee Theater has an elaborate interior that includes a domed ceiling and plaster moldings. The theater has been restored and is now a place for shows, movies, and the performances of the Knoxville Symphony and the Knoxville Opera Company. The entire building is now on the National Register.

Across Gay Street from the Burwell Building, you'll see the **Fouché Block**, one of the oldest structures remaining in the commercial center of the city, and next to it the **1875 Building**. The Fouché Building was used as a residence and office of Dr. John Fouché, a dentist, in the 1850s; it was converted to a business structure in 1875 with an addition in back and the construction of the 1875 Building. At this writing, these structures are abandoned, but there are proposals for historic renovation and reuse.

Continue north on Gay Street, crossing Clinch Avenue. On the northwest corner stands the **Holston National Bank Building** at 531 S. Gay, designed by John K. Peebles from Norfolk, Virginia, and built in 1912 in the Classical Revival style. This was later the Hamilton National Bank, one of many banks in the city center in the early part of the century. The Hamilton system at one time held over half of the city's assets. It is now the Charter Federal Building and is listed on the National Register.

On the northeast corner of Gay and Clinch, you'll find the old **Farragut Hotel Building** at 526-530 S. Gay, now used as an office building. The hotel opened in 1919 on the site of the Imperial Hotel that had burned in 1916. This was originally the site of the John H. Crozier House, which was the 1863 headquarters of General Ambrose Burnside when the city was occupied by Union forces during the Civil War. The hotel was named for Admiral David G. Farragut, who was born at Lowe's Ferry near Campbell Station to the west of Knoxville and who became famous in the Civil War Battle of Mobile Bay.

This block has several structures on the east side contributing to the Gay Street Historic District. Toward the middle, notice the old **S & W Cafeteria** at 516-520 S. Gay. The

Fouché Block (David Cann)

cafeteria was first located next to the Tennessee Theater, then was moved to this building, which was reconstructed in 1936 using a brick building that was already on the site. The S & W is a fine example of the Art Deco style with a multicolored, glazed terra cotta facade that has bronze and gold-leaf trim. Inside, it has checkered terrazzo floors, inlaid wood and marble and granite wall paneling, a curved staircase and walkway with bronze railings, and two 18 x 22-foot mirrors on either side of the lobby. Being in the heart of the city center and surrounded by shops, theaters, and hotels, the S & W was once the meeting place for Knoxville until it closed in 1981. It now stands empty.

At the end of the block, you'll find the Fidelity Bankers Trust building at 500-504 S. Gay, best known as the **Cowan, McClung and Company Building**. The structure was built in 1871, and then somewhat changed in 1929 to a Second Renaissance Revival style and is now on the National Register. Cowan, McClung and Company was formed around 1830 by James H. Cowan and C. J. and F. H. McClung who were merchants. The company prospered and was one of the largest wholesalers in dry goods through the turn of the century. Schriver's and Gateway Bookstore are shops housed in the building today.

Cross Union Avenue. On the west side of Gay Street is the old **Miller's Building** where Miller's Department Store was once located. The building was designed by R. F. Graf and Sons and built in 1905. It was later converted for office use. The building has a glass facade covering the original exterior.

On the east side of Gay Street, you'll find the **Kimball's Jewelers Building** at 428 S. Gay. A jewelry business has occupied the building since its construction at the turn of the century. In front of the building stands a large clock that was erected in 1915. There were several of these clocks along Gay Street at one time; this is the only one that remains.

Next to Kimball's, at 424 S. Gay Street, is **Woodruff's, Inc.**, which recently celebrated its 125th anniversary. The business was founded in 1865 by William Wallace Woodruff, an occupying Union soldier during the Civil War who chose to stay in Knoxville. Woodruff's was first a hardware store, at one time located in the Fouché Block. The current building was constructed in 1904 and has a manually operated elevator still in use.

Gay Street (David Cann)

In the intervening years the company grew into a home furnishings business that still has the traditional hardware department. The current president is a great-grandson of W. W. Woodruff.

As you continue north on Gay Street, you'll find on the left the old **S. H. Kress & Co. Store**, built about 1925. The old Kress chain of stores had its headquarters in Memphis. As the chain expanded, each of the stores took an architectural motif from part of the headquarters building. The store in Knoxville has a terra cotta front.

There were once other department stores along this stretch of Gay Street. In the 1960s, faculty and students from Knoxville College staged sit-in demonstrations at the lunch counters of these stores and in restaurants on Gay Street which eventually led to racial integration of public facilities in Knoxville. In 1897 a great fire destroyed many of the buildings on the east side of Gay Street north from Union Avenue. A second fire occurred in 1904. So the buildings on the east in this block have been constructed or restored since these fires.

At 312-314 S. Gay Street, you'll find the **Century Building**, a modern name given to the structure when it was rehabilitated for law offices in a project managed by the Brewer, Ingram, Fuller Architects, Inc. The building was originally the Haynes-Henson Shoe Company. The rehabilitation preserves the original appearance. The building to the right of the Century Building burned when a fire started in a restaurant that had located in the bottom floor.

At the end of this block, after passing Wall Street on the left, you'll reach Summit Hill Drive. This is the boundary of the Southern Terminal and Warehouse Historic District. You can cross Summit Hill Drive to begin the Southern Terminal and Warehouse District Walk, or you can turn left up Summit Hill to begin the Market Square Walk. To return to your starting point, simply turn around and walk back down Gay Street.

③ Southern Terminal and Warehouse District Walk

1.7 miles
Connections: Gay Street Walk, Market Square Walk, East Knoxville Tour

Attractions: This walk takes you through the Southern Terminal and Warehouse Historic District that includes "Old City."

Start: Begin at the corner of Gay Street and Summit Hill Drive.

Description: Walking north on Gay Street from Summit Hill Drive, you'll enter the **Southern Terminal and Warehouse District**, an historic district on the National Register of Historic Places. The district includes 72 structures on Gay, State, and Central Streets and Jackson and Vine Avenues.

This part of the City of Knoxville grew up around the railroad lines that led in and out of the northern end of the city. The first train arrived in Knoxville in 1855 as part of the East Tennessee and Georgia Railroad, which merged with the East Tennessee and Virginia Railroad after the Civil War to become the East Tennessee, Virginia, and Georgia Railroad Company. This rail line also absorbed the Knoxville and Ohio Railroad that had grown out of the Knoxville and Kentucky Railroad. Twenty-five years later the company was absorbed by the Southern Railway System. The other major line of the city was the Knoxville and Southern Railway System that merged in 1896 with the Marietta and North Georgia Railroad from Atlanta to form the Atlanta, Knoxville, and Northern Railroad. In 1902 the company was absorbed by the Louisville and Nashville Railroad Company.

The railroad was extremely important to the economy of the region. Store owners from the hinterlands could ride the railroad into the city to sell agricultural products they had acquired from the region's farmers and then purchase goods to take back to their stores. The region's products could then be shipped to such distant cities as Dalton, Chattanooga, Atlanta, Louisville, and Cincinnati. Knoxville thus became a major trade center of the Southeast with a large wholesale business that made it possible for the region's economy to participate in national markets.

Many mills and factories were attracted to Knoxville because of the rail lines. In 1874, there were about 50 wholesale houses in the city. By the end of the century, Knoxville was one of the four largest wholesale centers in the South, along with Atlanta, New Orleans, and Nashville.

In the years 1888 to 1894, many warehouses were constructed in this area of the city for storing goods. Processing companies also located here; JFG Coffee and White Lily Flour still operate out of this district. Small businesses grew up to cater to the traders coming to the city. The area once had many restaurants, saloons, nightclubs, and barber shops, often with living quarters upstairs.

On your walk, you'll first encounter Vine Avenue on the left, which once created the block with Central Street to your right; Summit Hill Drive, which has cut across Vine, is a relatively new street. Past Vine, continue north on Gay Street.

On the west side of the street, you'll find several jewelry and pawn shops occupying structures contributing to the historic district. You'll also find **Theatre Central** at 141 S. Gay, the location of a small theater group. At 131 S. Gay, stands **Harold's**, a kosher food deli that has been in operation for over 40 years and long ago became a Knoxville tradition.

On the east side of the street, notice the **Commerce Building** at 120-126 S. Gay Street. The brick structure was built around 1895 in the Italianate Commercial style. Tom's Place, now in the bottom right corner of the building, retains the original facade; there were once four such entrances. The other three stories still have the original facade.

Also on the east side of the street is the **Sterchi Building** at 114-116 S. Gay Street. The tall structure was built in the Commercial Style in 1921, designed by R. F. Graf and Sons. The Sterchi family immigrated from Switzerland in the mid-1800s. At the time, Switzerland was experiencing a severe economic depression, and many Swiss left their country to seek better opportunity in the United States. About 40,000 Swiss entered the U.S. in 1850-60, and around 20,000 entered in 1860-70. The Swiss were generally successful in their new homes. Descendents of the Sterchi family founded several businesses in Knox County, including a home furnishings business, Sterchi Brothers Furniture, for which the family name is perhaps best known. Over the years under the direction of J. G. Sterchi who acquired his brothers' interests in the company, Sterchi Brothers became a chain of sixty stores throughout the South. At one time, the building on Gay Street was the main business location.

To the left of the Sterchi Building, only a facade remains of a 1900 wholesale house that burned in 1974. You might walk by the facade and look through the window and door openings down to the ground level below. The street level was much lower at one time until the **Gay Street Viaduct** was built, which you can see just north. The viaduct was constructed in 1919 to bridge a marshy area that was called "Flag Pond" and to link the railroad/ warehouse district with the commercial district on Gay Street. When the viaduct was built, several of the buildings on this section of Gay Street had all or part of their ground floors covered by the elevated street. At the facade you can look down through what was the first floor and basement and subbasement. After the viaduct and the raising of the street, the store fronts of these buildings were constructed at the second floors, which had become the street-level floors.

It was in this vicinity at **110 S. Gay** that radio station WNOX once had its offices. The station is considered one of the oldest stations in the country, having started as WNAV in 1921.

At the southeast corner of Jackson Avenue and Gay Street, you'll see the **Emporium Building**, built in 1903 and incorporating the Second Renaissance Revival style. This structure housed another of the wholesale businesses.

At the corner of Jackson Avenue and Gay Street, you can see some of the old warehouses to the left on Jackson. From Jackson, continue north on Gay Street, walking across the Gay Street Viaduct over the railroad tracks.

You'll see the **Southern Railway Terminal** and adjacent office building to your right, set down on a level with the tracks. The building was designed by Frank P. Milburn and constructed

34

Southern Railway Terminal (David Cann)

in 1904 in the Dutch Revival style but with some Romanesque influences; it had a tall clock tower, which is now gone. A shed at the rear of the building kept passengers out of the rain as they were boarding the trains. The building was recently renovated by Bullock, Smith, and Partners to house several businesses, including the architectural firm's offices.

At the corner of Gay Street and Depot Avenue, turn right on Depot. You'll notice on the north side of Depot, the **Regas Restaurant** at 318 N. Gay Street. Founded in 1919 by the Regas family, the restaurant is known as one of the best in the South.

Continue on Depot, passing in front of the Southern Terminal Building, to Central Street. Turn right on Central; you'll pass between sections of the **White Lily Foods Company Plant**. Just past the plant, you'll cross railroad tracks where you'll need to use some caution because the sidewalk does not extend across the tracks and so the walking is a little rough.

On the south side of the tracks, you will be entering "**Old City**," a renovated portion of the Southern Terminal and Warehouse Historic District. Old City contains structures that have been rehabilitated to house various shops, restaurants, and commercial businesses with some upstairs residences, as in the old days.

On the right, you'll find **Hewgley's Music Shop**, a new construction that sits on what was a vacant lot. On the east side, you'll find **Lucille's** restaurant and bar, and then at the corner of Central and Jackson, **Patrick Sullivan's Saloon** at 100 North Central. Sullivan's was constructed about 1889 in the Eastlake style with a corner turret and is probably the best example in the Southeast of what a saloon was like at the time. The interior has been refurbished, and the saloon has reopened as a restaurant and bar. **Manhattan's**, another restaurant and bar, is across the intersection from Patrick Sullivan's. Each of these restaurants has live music at certain times.

At this intersection of Central and Jackson, you can wander either way on Jackson to see more of the structures contributing to the historic district. To the east on Jackson from Central, the old structures have been converted to offices, antique stores, and residences. Nearly all the buildings west on Jackson to Gay Street are contributing structures. You'll find **What the Dickens**

Jackson Street Warehouses

Bookseller on the right at 103 Jackson in an old tobacco and grain warehouse. The renovation is part of a project of developer Peter Calandruccio that includes the building to the left of the bookstore plus Hewgley's. Also on the north side of the street, you'll find the **Carhart Building** at 121 Jackson.

On the south side of Jackson in this block, the warehouse at **120-122 Jackson** was built around 1903 with a facade of yellow brick with red-brick trim and cast iron as part of the facade on the first story. The red-brick warehouse at **124 Jackson**, built about 1894, has a facade with cast iron on two stories. The building at 130-132 Jackson will soon be rehabilitated into the **Jackson Square Condominiums**. Then at 200 Jackson, you'll find part of the **JFG Coffee** plant that is connected by a tube overhead to more of the plant on the north side of the street. The long shed on the north side that was once part of the railroad operations is also part of the JFG complex.

Return to Central. Continuing south, you'll pass several buildings in the process of renovation with occasional shops, offices, and condominiums. At 113 Central, on the right, the **Tri-City Barber College** has been in operation at this location since at least 1911, making it perhaps the oldest barber school in continuous operation in the country; the building dates from before 1900. On the left side of the street, you'll also find **Amigo's**, a Mexican restaurant, and then on the right farther down the block, the **131 Central Deli**.

At the end of the block, you'll arrive at the corner of Central and Summit Hill Drive. This was once the corner of Vine Avenue and Central and was the site of the Knoxville Riot of 1919 that emphasized the tension between the races at the time. Both blacks and Appalachian whites had moved into the city seeking jobs and economic opportunity. Hostility between the two working groups rose to the surface when a black was accused of killing a white woman. Although the accused was moved to Chattanooga, a white mob gathered and stormed the Knoxville jail on the south end of town, confiscated the whiskey that had been stored there from raids during prohibition, and destroyed the jail and the sheriffs' adjoining house. The mob then headed for Vine Avenue, where blacks were supposedly gathering; on the way the mob broke into stores, searching for guns. Guardsmen of the Tennessee Fourth Infantry arrived to keep the peace, but when the mob got to the corner of Vine and Central, shooting broke out, with the whites and the guardsmen firing at blacks who fired back. The next day, more guardsmen arrived and the fighting was stopped. At least one black was killed and one guardsman; although 36 whites were arrested, none was convicted.

Across Summit Hill Drive on the corner, stands **Kings Row**, an older structure built about 1900 that has been renovated into offices. The **Willingham Garrets** are adjacent. From this corner, you can begin the East Knoxville driving tour to the left on Summit Hill Drive. To complete this walk, turn right up Summit Hill Drive. After State Street joins Summit Hill on the left, you'll see some of the buildings that contribute to the Gay Street Commercial Historic District, including the **Bacon & Co.** buildings constructed around 1900.

At the end of the block at the northeast corner of Summit Hill and Gay Street, you'll find a small park, the **East Tennessee Tribute to Country Music** that features a sculpture of the treble clef. Knoxville is considered the birthplace of country music. WNOX in Knoxville was the first to broadcast country music, including live shows where performers such as Roy Acuff and Chet Atkins got their start.

At this corner, you'll be at the end of the Gay Street Walk. You can continue west on Summit Hill Drive to begin the Market Square Walk.

4 Market Square Walk

1.3 miles
Connections: Gay Street Walk, Southern Terminal and
Warehouse District Walk, World's Fair Park Walk,
Mechanicsville Tour

Attractions: This loop walk takes you through the Market
Square Commercial and Historic District, Krutch Park, and by
Old City Hall.

Start: Begin at the corner of Gay Street and Summit Hill Drive.

Description: Walking west, uphill, on Summit Hill Drive, you'll
come to the **Radisson Hotel** on the north and, on the south, the
TVA Towers of the Tennessee Valley Authority, built in the
1970s. A federal agency that is one of the largest utilities in the
world, TVA provides electrical power throughout the Tennessee
River Valley region using coal, nuclear, and hydroelectric plants.

Mandated by Congress to harness the Tennessee River and
its tributaries for the benefit of the valley, TVA built 14 major
dams from its founding in 1933 to 1979. Through its programs,
the agency has brought flood control, navigation, electricity, and
a measure of economic improvement to the region.

The Tellico Dam on the Little Tennessee River south of
Knoxville was the last dam TVA constructed. In the 1970s a
much publicized controversy over building the Tellico Dam
centered around the extinction of an endangered species that
lived in the river, a small fish called the "snail darter." The real
issues were flood control, electric power, and lakeside development versus the concerns of conservationists about submerging
one of the last undammed rivers, flooding farmland, and drown-
ing what was the sacred valley of the Overhill Cherokee Indians.
The debate went all the way to the U.S. Supreme Court, which
ruled that the Tellico Dam violated the Endangered Species Act
and could not be completed. But Tennessee's Senators and
Congressmen managed to pass a bill exempting the Tellico Dam

from the law. The dam was closed and Tellico Lake formed in 1979.

Turn south at the TVA Towers; walk up the stairs and cross the plaza between the two buildings. At the far end of the plaza you'll be overlooking **Market Square**, a historic commercial district on the National Register of Historic Places. The district includes 18 contributing structures, principally those on both sides of the square that stretches before you. These buildings were constructed between 1875 and 1925.

Knoxville originally had a market house on the bank of the Tennessee River to receive farm produce shipped by boat. The market was moved several times until a public market house was built on this location in the center of the square in 1854 on land donated to the city by Joseph A. Mabry and William G. Swan. Mabry and Swan were brothers-in-law; Mabry became president of the Knoxville and Kentucky Railroad, and Swan became mayor of the city in 1855. In addition to the market house, which was replaced in 1897, the square contained a building constructed on its north end that was the City Hall for a time. Around the square were retail stores, bakeries, butcher shops, and coffee-houses. While the Gay Street District was the financial and commercial center of the city, and the Warehouse District was the wholesale center with outreach to the region, Market Square was the center for the local economy before the exodus to the suburbs.

When the market house was damaged by a fire in 1960 and demolished, downtown businessmen took the opportunity to create a Market Square Mall in an attempt to draw the retail trade back from the suburbs by mimicking the malls that had grown up on the outskirts of the city. But the project was just a series of canopies covering the old store fronts and a canopied market-place in the center. Today the mall concept is gone, and the site is now simply the Market Square, where an open-air pavilion built in 1984 provides a place for farmers to set up stands for selling produce and flowers and for live music performances. The design for the pavilion was the result of a design competition won by the architectural firm of Bullock, Smith, and Partners.

As you walk down the steps into Market Square, notice the TVA Fountain, which was designed to give the impression of movement from the TVA Towers through Market Square. The

Market Square

impression of water flowing toward the Tennessee River is reinforced by the stream flowing through Krutch Park at the southern end of the square.

The Market Square today contains numerous shops and restaurants that principally serve the lunchtime crowd. In addition to several delis and food shops, the restaurants include on the west side of the square **The Blakely Cafe** and **The Soup Kitchen**, and on the east side, **Up Town Cafe and Bakery**, and around the corner on Wall Avenue at the northern end of the square, **Perry's**.

At the far end of Market Square, you'll find the old **Kerns Bakery Building**, designed by Joseph F. Baumann and built around 1872 and now on the National Register; it houses the Soup Kitchen and Blakely restaurants. On the other side of Union Avenue, on the southwest corner, stands the **Arnstein Building**, built in 1905 to contain offices and the Max B. Arnstein department store; it is still an office/commercial building and contains the headquarters of Whittle Communications until their new complex on Main Avenue is completed.

At the southeast corner of Market Square, you'll find **Krutch Park**, constructed in 1983 with funds donated by Charles Krutch, a TVA photographer from 1931-56 who recorded the beginnings of the agency in his nationally recognized photography. His brother was the writer Joseph Wood Krutch, and their uncle was Charles Christopher Krutch, a noted landscape artist whose favorite subject was the Great Smoky Mountains, a national park to the southeast of Knoxville. Krutch Park is designed to recreate the feel of the forests of the Great Smoky Mountains.

Take a walk through the park, and when you emerge from the southern end on Clinch Avenue, you'll be facing the **U.S. Post Office and Custom House**, designed by Alfred B. Mullett and built in 1873 in the Second Renaissance Revival style with local Tennessee marble. The building, at 314 W. Clinch Avenue, was enlarged by an east wing in 1910. When the new post office on Main Avenue opened in 1934, the old post office was used as offices for many years by the Tennessee Valley Authority, but eventually the building was declared surplus and transferred to the Knox County Public Library System. Now it is the location of the library's East Tennessee Historical Center that maintains

Krutch Park (David Cann)

44

the Knox County Archives and the Calvin M. McClung Historical Collection, which contains information and records on East Tennessee and the state including the papers of prominent Tennesseans such as William Blount, John Sevier, and Andrew Johnson. The historical collection is named for Calvin Morgan McClung, a wholesale industrialist who gathered much of the material that formed the basis of the collection; the papers were donated by his wife, Barbara Adair McClung, to the library in 1921. Both the archives and the McClung Collection are open to the public. The building also contains the offices of the East Tennessee Historical Society, and plans call for the establishment of an East Tennessee regional historical museum on the first floor.

Today this building is usually referred to as just the "Custom House." Although there was little, if any, international barge traffic on the Tennessee River that required the paying of customs, when a post office building was needed, "Custom House" was added to the name as a gimmick to easily solicit federal funds from the U.S. Congress who associated the word "custom" with revenues. On the corner and west side of the building, you can see what were the original entrances to the building, worn thresholds below what are now windows.

Adjacent to the Custom House on the east is the **Fouché Block**, which faces Gay Street. Turn right on Clinch Avenue. If the street has not yet been upgraded, you'll notice through cracks in the asphalt the tracks of the old streetcar system that once ran throughout the city. In 1876 it was a mule-drawn car; by 1893 it was an electric trolley car. Expansion of the streetcar to the outskirts of the city provided easy access from outside the city and so permitted the beginning of the growth of the suburbs that would essentially drain the city core of its residents. The streetcar system was converted to buses in the 1940s. Today trolley-style buses provide transportation from outlying parking centers that make peripheral parking more accessible and thus reduce the need for parking downtown.

You'll pass on the left at 414 Clinch a building faced with sandstone that was originally the **Morris Plan Bank** and today still houses bank offices. At the corner of Clinch and Walnut Street, you'll arrive at the **YWCA Building** at 420 Clinch. Built in 1925 in the Neoclassical Revival style, the building has been determined to be eligible for National Register listing. On the northwest corner of the intersection, stands the **Althea**, built about 1915 as an apartment building and now renovated for offices. Turn south on Walnut one block to Church Avenue and turn right on Church.

On your left will be the **Lawson McGhee Library** at 500 W. Church, the main library for the Knox County Public Library System, designed by McCarty and Bullock. You'll pass the **Downtown Hilton** on the right and reach Locust Street. Turn right on Locust. On your left, you'll find **Hess's Department Store**, which had been Miller's and before that Rich's Department Store. The building of this department store in the mid-1950s was one of the first moves in the gradual relocation of retail stores out of the central business district along Gay Street, which once had such stores as J. C. Penney, Miller's, S. H. Kress, and S. H. George, in addition to McClellan's which still operates on Gay Street.

On the southeast corner of Locust and Clinch Avenue, beside Hess's Department Store, you'll find a covered walkway that will carry you west over Henley Street to the World's Fair Park. This is the beginning of the World's Fair Park Walk.

On the northwest corner of Locust and Clinch, you'll notice the **Knoxville YMCA Building** at 605 Clinch Avenue. Built in 1928, the building is now on the National Register. It is slated for restoration, with condominiums to be in the top floors.

Continue north one block to Union Avenue. You'll pass the **Masonic Temple**, which was originally the home of Charles McClung McGhee, designed by Joseph Baumann and built about 1872. McGhee, a financier and businessman in coal and railroads, was a University of Tennessee trustee and treasurer who established the Lawson McGhee Library in 1885 in memory of his daughter May Lawson McGhee Williams, who died in 1883; the library became part of the public system in 1917.

Next on your left will be **Kendrick Place Townhouses** at 600-610 Union Avenue. Built about 1890 and at one time called "Masonic Court," the townhouses are some of the last remaining rowhouses in Knoxville. Brick, two-story, attached structures in the Victorian Vernacular style, the townhouses are representa-

46

Kendrick Place (David Cann)

tive of residences that were once part of the downtown area before the more economically advantaged fled to the suburbs. The trend toward out-migration is now gradually being reversed by the revitalization of the city center and the renovation of such structures into apartments and condominiums. Kendrick Place is one of the projects of Kristopher Kendrick, a developer primarily interested in old city restoration who has done much to revitalize Knoxville's city center. Kristopher and Company projects have also included the Lord Lindsey and The River House on Hill Avenue, The Stuart and The Cunningham on Market Street, Kings Row and The Willingham Garrets on Summit Hill Drive, and several projects along Central Street in "Old City," including Patrick Sullivan's Saloon.

At this location, Union Avenue swings around Kendrick Place. To the east, Union joins the southern end of Market Square. If you walk this section of Union, the second building you pass on the right will be the **Sprankle Building** that houses the Pembroke Apartments and shops and offices built about 1925 (notice the copper cornice and canopy trim) and on the left the **Daylight Building** built around 1925 for offices. The old **Park Hotel** sits on the southeast corner of Union and Walnut, built 1880-90. The hotel building has shops facing Union. Next to it stands a commercial building constructed about 1890, and then the **Grand Union** office building constructed about 1925 and recently renovated (again notice the copper canopy trim). On the north side of Union, you'll see the **Kerns Bakery Building** that on this side contains **The Blakely Hotel**.

From the junction of Union and Locust, walk just north of Kendrick Place and turn left on Union. At the end of the block, you'll be at Henley Street. On your left is **Chesapeake's**, a seafood restaurant, and next door you'll find the **Knoxville Convention and Visitors Bureau** at 500 Henley where you can get detailed information on what to see and do in the Knoxville area. This 1920s building is being considered for demolition to make way for a tunnel that will emerge at this point from I-275.

To complete the loop back to Market Square, turn north on Henley. You'll see the old **L&N Railroad Station** across Henley that's included in the World's Fair Park Walk. At the end of the block, you'll reach the intersection of four primary streets—

Henley on the south, Summit Hill Drive to the east, Western Avenue to the west, and Broadway to the north. West on Western, you can reach the Mechanicsville Neighborhood. North on Broadway, you'll find Emory Place, Old North Knoxville, Oakwood, and finally Fountain City.

Turn right on Summit Hill Drive to complete this walk. Across Summit Hill Drive, you'll see the **Old City Hall**. The building complex served as Knoxville's City Hall from 1925 to 1980 when the new City-County Building opened on Hill Avenue. The buildings were restored to their original appearance in 1983 and now house offices for TVA. The several buildings in the complex were built between 1848 and 1905 as the Tennessee School for the Deaf, which relocated to the Island Home area of South Knoxville in 1924. The primary building was constructed in 1848-51 in the Greek Revival style by Jacob Newman. During the Civil War, the school served as a hospital for the Confederates until 1863 when it became a hospital for Union soldiers.

On the right you'll see the headquarters of the **Knoxville Fire Department** with a glass showcase on the lawn with artifacts that represent the history of the Department. The exhibit includes one of the first steam-pump engines used by the Fire Department. A memorial on the grounds honors those who have died fighting fires. The sculpture of a fireman with a child on his arm was a memorial to William Maxey and John Dunn, two North Knoxville firemen who died in 1904 fighting a fire on Gay Street. The sculpture originally topped a double horse trough in front of the Old Knox County Courthouse on Main Avenue.

After the Fire Department, turn left at Locust Street across Summit Hill Drive to the Old City Hall. Continue east on Summit Hill to Walnut Street and turn left along the side of the **Church of the Immaculate Conception**, which faces Vine Avenue. Designed by Baumann Brothers and completed in 1886 in the Victorian Gothic style at the top of Summit Hill, the church served the Catholic congregation in Knox County that had organized in 1854. At this location, a Union battery called "Battery Wiltsie" stretched along this ridge during the Union occupation of the city.

Complete your tour by returning on Walnut to Summit Hill Drive and turning east to the TVA Towers.

5 World's Fair Park Walk

1.0 mile

Connections: Market Square Walk, University of Tennessee
Campus Walk, Fort Sanders Walk, Bicentennial Park

Attractions: This tour takes you through the former site of the
1982 World's Fair, past the new Knoxville Museum of Art, and
into the historic Maplehurst community.

Start: Begin at the corner of Hess's Department Store at Locust
Street and Clinch Avenue where a pedestrian bridge takes you
west over Henley Street.

Description: What began as Energy Expo '82 and eventually
grew into the 1982 World's Fair with the theme "Energy Turns
the World" was the beginning of revitalization for the city center
of Knoxville. The fair provided the opportunity to rebuild the
lower Second Creek area on the western edge of the city center
and the incentive to improve other city facilities.

The lower Second Creek area originally consisted of railway
yards and a run-down neighborhood. In the late '70s, when an
energy exposition was first suggested, most of the residential
buildings had been torn down, but the blighted area continued to
be a barrier separating the city center from the University of
Tennessee to the west. Some citizens of the city were initially
opposed to the idea of Knoxville hosting a World's Fair because
of their fear of higher taxes to fund the construction and increased
traffic congestion from a multitude of visitors. But to the propo-
nents, the fair seemed the answer to the city's problems. The fair
would revitalize the inner city, link the city center with the
university community, and be the justification for numerous city
improvements, including revamping the road and interstate highway system that had made traveling through Knoxville infamous.

To create the fair site, a park-like setting was constructed
along the lower Second Creek. A U.S. pavilion, exhibition hall,
and structures for the participating countries were built. The

Sunsphere that became the symbol of the fair was erected. The '82 World's Fair opened on May 1 and ran through October 31.

Years after the fair, the expected commercial, residential, and recreational facilities that were supposed to fill the site have not appeared as expected. Yet, the fair site, now a park, provides a much needed open area in the city center and a meeting place for outdoor concerts and other gatherings. The site also has a number of offices and restaurants.

Crossing Henley on the pedestrian bridge, you'll come to the parking garage of Hess's Department Store on the left, which connects by a subterranean passageway to the store on the east side of Henley. The bridge turns right, and you'll descend stairs to the ground level at the **Holiday Inn Downtown** and state offices occupying the upper floors of the **Knoxville Convention and Exhibition Center**.

From the pedestrian bridge, the **Clinch Avenue Viaduct** stretches to the west. Clinch Avenue was once a main artery to the west, but this section was permanently closed to traffic with the construction of the World's Fair site. The viaduct, built in 1905, has 15 concrete-filled spandrel arch spans and is the oldest known vehicular concrete arch bridge in the state.

Just to the left of the beginning of the viaduct, you'll see the **Sunsphere**, which was a restaurant during the fair. At this writing, the structure is unoccupied, but plans call for offices to be located inside and a restaurant to open. When that happens, you will once again be able to ride the elevator up into the golden ball for rooftop views of the city.

From the Sunsphere, you can descend stairs to the ground level below the viaduct and walk the grounds of the World's Fair Park. But to get an elevated view, walk across the Clinch Avenue Viaduct. On the right, you'll see the Convention and Exhibition Center where occasional exhibitions are still held and across Second Creek the **Court of Flags** where the flags of participating countries were flown during the fair. At the far north end of the park, stands the old **L&N Railroad Station**, consisting of the elaborate passenger station, designed by Richard Monford and built in 1904-05 and, to the left, the freight depot, originally built in 1904 and rebuilt in 1922 after a fire. The L&N Railroad maintained offices here until the early 1980s. The passenger

Sunsphere (David Cann)

station now houses offices and **Ruby Tuesday's** and the **L&N Seafood Grill** restaurants. The freight depot now contains offices and **The Butcher Shop** restaurant. At that end of the park, also notice the **Western Avenue Viaduct**; constructed in 1909-10, this is one of the first continuous concrete deck girders in the U.S.

If you explore the grounds of the World's Fair Park, you should examine the L&N passenger station in detail; basically Victorian in style, it has stained glass windows in front and an ascending stairway in back. If you walk to that end of the park, you'll also find sitting under the Western Avenue Viaduct a brick building that was the original foundry of the **Knoxville Iron Company**. Founded around 1868 by former Union Army Captain H. S. Chamberlain and several Welsh ironmasters, the company manufactured bar iron, railroad spikes, and nails among other iron products and became one of the leading employers in the city. The company moved from this location in the early 1900s. On the National Register, the building, which is all that is left of the Knoxville Iron Company, was renovated for the World's Fair; it recently reopened as **Ella Guru's**, a restaurant and lounge known for its live music.

To the left of the Clinch Avenue Viaduct, you'll see to the west the open-air **Tennessee Amphitheater** where performances were held during the fair and are still held today. At the south end of the park, across the lake, stands the **United States Pavilion** that housed various exhibits and demonstrations during the fair. It now stands unused. Various proposals for using the pavilion as a museum have failed, mostly because of the cost of renovating the structure. The building is now slated for demolition unless a use for the building can be found. Either way, some use needs to be found for the **Thomas Humes House**. Dr. Thomas W. Humes, the son of Thomas Humes who had the Lamar House built, was rector of the St. John's Episcopal Church and later president of East Tennessee University from 1865 to 1883, during which it become the University of Tennessee. The Humes House, built in the 1840s, stood on Cumberland Avenue in what is now the courtyard of St. John's Episcopal Cathedral until 1983. When it was threatened with demolition, Bill Powell, a young man interested in historic preservation in Knoxville, with the help of others, disassembled the house and stored it in the U.S. Pavilion for some future use. It is still there.

Proceed to the west end of the viaduct. You'll find the **Candy Factory** on the right. Built in the early 1900s, the building was the second location of Littlefield and Steere Candy Company, which had been on S. Gay Street. The factory was used as a warehouse in the mid-part of the century and was then renovated for use during the World's Fair when it housed restaurants. It now contains various shops, exhibits, art galleries, and the offices of the Knoxville Arts Council and The City Ballet.

Just to the north is the new **Knoxville Museum of Art**, completed in 1990 and faced with Tennessee marble. In addition to the present four galleries and a great hall, the museum will eventually have two gardens, one featuring sculpture and the other serving as an outdoor classroom.

Just west of the Candy Factory and Museum of Art, you'll find several Victorian houses on 11th Street that along with the Candy Factory form an **Arts Center**. These late-1800 Victorian homes were renovated during the World's Fair to house exhibits and restaurants. Now they provide exhibit and workshop space for local artists to work, sell, and demonstrate their arts and crafts. You can enter the Victorian house complex by taking the walkway across from the Candy Factory that has the white railing. At this point on 11th Street, you are also at the beginning of the Fort Sanders Neighborhood Walk.

From the Candy Factory and the Victorian houses, walk south on 11th Street. Cross Cumberland where you can connect with the University of Tennessee Campus Walk to the right.

To continue on the World's Fair Park Walk, turn left on Cumberland. You'll cross over Second Creek and see on the right the entrance to a parking lot that during the World's Fair was a connector between an amusement park to the south and the main fair site you have just left. There remains a bridge walkway over Cumberland Avenue that connects the two areas, but it is now closed because a train also uses the bridge. You'll find in this parking area a small park on the right along Second Creek. At the far end of the parking area, you can by a winding ramp walk down to Second Creek and walk under Neyland Drive to connect with Bicentennial Park.

11th Street Victorian Houses (David Cann)

Continue east on Cumberland. At the corner of Poplar Place, turn right and then left when you get to Hill Avenue. At Maplehurst Court, turn right into the **Maplehurst Park**, a grouping of residential buildings constructed from 1910 to 1930 in the Mission, Tudor Revival, Bungalow, Prairie, and Spanish Colonial Revival styles. Several of these structures were originally built as apartment houses and are still used for apartments today. This area has been recommended for an historic district on the National Register. The residential park took its name from a large house that was first built here around 1870; it was called initially "Riverlawn," but a later owner changed the name to "Maplehurst." The house burned while owned by a university fraternity.

From Maplehurst Park, continue east on Hill Avenue. Notice at 800 Hill Avenue **The Middleton**, an inn built about 1910 as a residence. At the corner of Henley Street, turn left, headed north. In this block bounded by Hill, Henley, and Cumberland, you'll find the **Church Street United Methodist Church** built in 1930-31 using Crab Orchard sandstone. The church was designed by Barber & McMurry, with John Russell Pope of New York as consulting architect. The church was originally located on Church Street, but that structure burned in 1928 and the new structure on Henley was built.

Continue north on Henley to the pedestrian bridge over Henley to Hess's Department Store. You'll notice that on this side the department store is emblazoned with "The University of Tennessee," for the **University of Tennessee Conference Center** and other administrative offices of the university that now also occupy the building. Here you can recross Henley on the bridge to return to your starting point.

Maplehurst Park (David Cann)

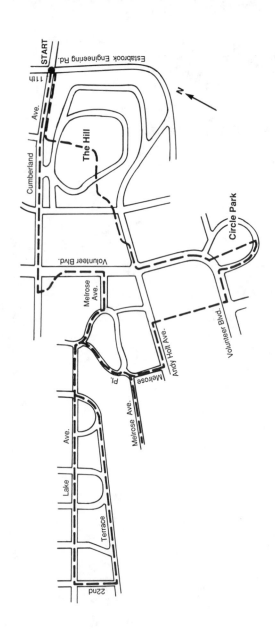

The University of Tennessee Campus

58

⑥ The University of Tennessee Campus Walk

3.2 miles
Connections: World's Fair Park Walk, Fort Sanders Walk

Attractions: This walk through part of the University of Tennessee Campus takes you by buildings that date from the early part of the century.

Start: Begin at the corner of Cumberland Avenue and 11th Street, which is also the southwest corner of the World's Fair Park Walk. From here you can also turn north up 11th Street to the beginning of the Fort Sanders Neighborhood Walk.

Description: Only three years after the founding of Knoxville, Blount College was established in 1794 to educate the young people of the growing community. Samuel Carrick, the minister of the First Presbyterian Church, was appointed the president of the college. In spite of Carrick's church affiliation, the school was nonsectarian, unusual at a time when most schools were denominational. The trustees of the new college included such notables as William Blount, for whom the college was named, John Sevier, James White, John Adair, and F. A. Ramsey.

The college consisted of one building constructed in 1795 on land donated by James White that is today the site of the Burwell Building in the city center. The college offered English grammar, geography, logic, philosophy, astronomy, rhetoric, Latin, and Greek. Carrick taught all the courses. William E. Parker was the only person known to have completed a degree during the college's 13-year history.

In 1807, the school name was changed to "East Tennessee College" to put it in a more favorable position to receive a land grant of former Cherokee lands that were to be used to support education. The new college remained on the site at Clinch and Gay, and Carrick remained its President. Two years later, Carrick unexpectedly died, and with no one to operate the institution and because of a shortage of funds, the trustees apparently kept the college closed from 1809 until 1820 when it merged with Hampden-Sidney Academy and opened with that institution's president in charge. The two schools separated in 1826, with East Tennessee College moving from its original site to a hill west of the city center that was known first as "Barbara Hill," after William Blount's daughter, but later became known as "College Hill" and is today referred to as simply "The Hill." A building to house the college was completed in 1828, called "College Hall" or "Old College." Other buildings were soon added for dormitories.

In 1840 the college became East Tennessee University. During the Civil War, the buildings were occupied first by Confederate and then Union troops. College Hall was used as a hospital.

After the war, the university operated for a short time out of the buildings of the Tennessee School for the Deaf in the city center. Once the breastworks were removed from the university and the buildings were made fit for occupation, the university returned to The Hill. Finally in 1879, the institution became the University of Tennessee, Knoxville, that today has an enrollment of 25,000 students on a campus of 288 acres plus a 130-acre agricultural campus and the University of Tennessee Medical Center at Knoxville. The university has 230 structures that include academic and support buildings, athletic facilities, and apartments and residence halls.

At the corner of Cumberland and 11th Street, you will be standing at the bottom of The Hill, the site to which East Tennessee College moved and from which the University of Tennessee has expanded westward. Begin ascending The Hill by walking west on the south side of Cumberland. You'll soon come to a long set of stairs on your left. Ascend the stairs to Circle Drive. Cross the drive and keep ascending along a walkway that leads to **Ayres Hall**, which dominates The Hill. Completed in 1921, the Collegiate Gothic building was named for Brown Ayres, President of the university from 1904 to 1919. It had been Ayres's dream to have a large building crowning The Hill. Unfortunately, College Hall, along with other of the original
60

Ayres Hall (David Cann)

university buildings, was torn down to make room for the new building.

Still, the crest of The Hill has some of the oldest buildings on campus and has been proposed as an historic district for the National Register of Historic Places. To see these other buildings on Circle Drive, enter Ayres Hall and walk through to emerge on the other side. Counterclockwise from Ayres Hall you'll find the **Austin Peay Building**. This was originally the site of the Carnegie Library, built in 1911. When the larger James D. Hoskins Library was constructed across Cumberland Avenue in 1931, the Carnegie Library was torn down and an administration building constructed. It was later remodeled and enlarged and was named the "Austin Peay Memorial Administration Building" in honor of Tennessee's governor from 1923 to 1927 who was a supporter of the university. In 1974, the building was remodeled into offices for the psychology department.

Next to the Austin Peay Building stands the **Hesler Biology Building**, designed by Barber & McMurry and built in 1935 and named for L. R. Hesler, who was dean of the College of Liberal Arts, 1934-58. Adjacent to Hesler stands the **Nielsen Physics Building**, designed by Barber & McMurry and completed in 1962; Alvin H. Nielsen was a physics professor and dean of Liberal Arts. Before construction of this new physics building, the adjacent **Geology and Geography Building**, designed in the Collegiate Gothic style by Barber & McMurry and built in 1928, had been the physics and geology building.

South College completes the circle. East, West, North, and South College buildings once ringed The Hill, but only South College remains. Built in 1872, it is the oldest building on campus. Originally a men's dormitory, it was later a classroom building and an administration building. It was remodeled in 1908, and then in 1989 the building was renovated to house the university's Science Alliance, which promotes research and educational collaborations between the university and Oak Ridge National Laboratory located in Oak Ridge to the west of Knoxville.

Behind South College stands **Dabney/Buehler Hall**, the chemistry building, constructed in 1928 with later additions, named for Charles Dabney, university President, 1887-1904, and

Calvin Buehler, a former head of the Chemistry Department. Farther down The Hill stands the **Dougherty Engineering Building** on Estabrook Engineering Road, completed in 1963 and named for a former dean of the College of Engineering. Both buildings were designed by Barber & McMurry.

Descend from The Hill to the west down the walkway between the Austin Peay and Hesler Buildings. You'll find just beyond them, **Turner House**, originally built in 1892 as a residence for Prof. George Mellen. The house was later bought by the university and rented to law Prof. Charles Turner as a residence.

From Turner House, take the pedestrian bridge to the left that passes over Stadium Drive to the plaza on top of a parking garage. From the beginning of the bridge, you'll be able to see just to the left the **Alumni Memorial Gymnasium**, designed by Barber & McMurry and completed in 1934; varsity basketball was played here until Stokely Athletic Center was constructed. You'll also see **Neyland Stadium** rising behind the Alumni Gym; the stadium surrounds **Shields-Watkins Field** where varsity football games are played. The field is named for W. S. Shields and his wife Alice Watkins Shields who donated money to prepare the field. The 91,110-seat stadium, the second largest college stadium in the country, is named for Robert R. Neyland, UT head football coach, 1926-52, and athletic director, 1952-62. The first part of the stadium was constructed in 1921; there have since been 12 additions, the latest in 1987.

On the other side of Neyland Stadium, hidden from view, is one of the few buildings dating from before 1900, **Estabrook Hall**, built in 1898 with later additions and named for Joseph Estabrook, President of the university, 1834-50. You can reach Estabrook Hall by taking Middle Drive, which runs in front of the Alumni Gym, and then Lower Drive, which passes between Neyland Stadium and Perkins Hall. Estabrook now contains several engineering programs.

After crossing the pedestrian bridge and walking to the far end of the plaza, bear left and you'll emerge on Andy Holt Avenue; Holt was university President, 1959-70. Turn right, and you'll find on your right the **Glocker Business Administration Building**, designed by Bealer and Wilhoite and constructed in

1951 and named for Theodore W. Glocker, first dean of the College of Business Administration.

At the corner with Volunteer Boulevard, you'll see across the street the **John C. Hodges Library**, completed in 1987 with McCarty, Bullock, & Holsaple the principal architects. The 1.7 million-volume library is the main campus library. The construction of the new library completely incorporated the earlier John C. Hodges Undergraduate Library constructed in 1969. Hodges, a UT English professor and head of the English Department, 1938-62, wrote *Harbrace College Handbook*, the standard English grammar text used in colleges across the country.

Turn left on Volunteer Boulevard, crossing Andy Holt Avenue. On your left you'll reach the **Claxton Education Building**, built in 1957 with a 1982 addition on the far side; Barber & McMurry designed the original building, named for Philander P. Claxton, a former head of the College of Education who became U.S. Commissioner of Education, 1911-21. Across the street, you'll see the **McClung Plaza and Tower** and the **Humanities and Social Sciences Building**, designed by Painter, Weeks, and McCarty and built in 1967; the complex contains offices and classrooms of the College of Liberal Arts. The plaza bears a statue of Europa and the Bull. The McClung Plaza and Tower are named for Hugh L. and Ella L. McClung, the parents of Mrs. Thomas Berry, who made a donation for the construction of the complex.

Just past the **College of Nursing Building** on your left, constructed in 1977, head into Circle Park past the statue of **The Volunteer** that holds a flame aloft. The school nickname is "The Volunteers," which came from Tennessee being "The Volunteer State," a name that was given to Tennessee because of the large numbers of Tennessee men who volunteered to fight in the War of 1812 and the Mexican War.

A brick path takes you through **Circle Park**. You'll find along Circle Park Drive to the left the **Communications and University Extension Building**, designed by Painter, Weeks, and McCarty and constructed in 1969, which houses among many offices those of the University of Tennessee Press and the Tennessee Newspaper Hall of Fame. The half of the complex straight ahead is the **Student Services Building** and rising

64

McClung Tower with Europa and the Bull (David Cann)

behind it **Andy Holt Tower**, designed by Bruce McCarty and Associates and completed in 1973.

When you emerge on Circle Park Drive, walk to the right. You'll find the **McClung Museum**, built in 1962-63 with a bequest from Ellen McClung Green as a memorial to her father Frank H. McClung, who had been part of the Cowan, McClung and Company wholesale house and earlier had been a student at East Tennessee University. The museum, designed by Barber & McMurry, preserves and exhibits objects in anthropology, archeology, art and architecture, geology, local history, and natural history.

After the museum, you will emerge from Circle Park back on Volunteer Boulevard; turn left to the corner of Lake Loudoun Boulevard. From this corner, you can see far to the left part of the new beige **Thompson-Boling Assembly Center and Arena** to the southeast. Designed by Joseph Goodstein, the 24,535-seat arena where varsity basketball is now played is the largest on-campus arena in the country. It was named for B. Ray Thompson, who contributed to the project, and Edward J. Boling, university President, 1970-88. Across Lake Loudoun Boulevard stands **Gibbs Hall**, a dormitory built in 1961, designed by Baumann and Baumann and named for Bill Gibbs, an assistant basketball coach who died in a plane crash. It was extensively renovated in 1987-88. To the left of Gibbs, you'll see the new **Neyland-Thompson Sports Center**, a football practice facility that also houses the university's Football Hall of Fame. On the far side of Gibbs Halls, you'll find the **William B. Stokely Athletic Center**, where varsity basketball was played until the new arena was completed. To construct the Stokely Center, a field house built in the late 1950s was expanded using a gift from W. B. Stokely, Jr.; the design was by Barber & McMurry.

At this corner, cross Volunteer Boulevard to the **Art and Architecture Building**, designed by McCarty, Bullock, & Holsaple and constructed in 1981. To the west is the **Music Building**, designed by Barber & McMurry and constructed in 1966, where you can attend the university music arts series. You'll find a walkway on the east side of the Art and Architecture Building that will take you behind the Humanities and Social Sciences Building.

After passing along the side of the Art and Architecture Building, you'll see to the left of the walkway two theaters. The **Carousel Theater**, built in 1952 as a theater-in-the-round, can become an open-air theater by removing the walls. The **Clarence Brown Theater**, designed by Bruce McCarty and Associates and built in 1970, was named to honor the famous Hollywood director who was an alumnus of the university and who helped fund the construction. The public is encouraged to attend the productions at both theaters.

At the end of the walkway, you'll be at Andy Holt Avenue. Across the street stands **Melrose Hall**, a dormitory built in 1946 and designed by Barber & McMurry. Cross Andy Holt Avenue and turn left; at the next corner stands **Hess Hall**, a Baumann and Baumann design built in 1960.

This tour covers only part of the UT Campus, which extends far to the west. If you were to continue west, you would find the **Physical Education Building** and the **Tom Black Track and Recreation Area**, several dormitories, the **Student Aquatic Center**, and to the southwest, **Fraternity Park Drive**. Farther west, the Agricultural Campus contains over 20 structures, including **Morgan Hall**, completed in 1921 in the Collegiate Gothic design, named for university President Harcourt A. Morgan, 1919-34, and proposed for the National Register. Even farther to the southwest, by passing over the Tennessee River on the Alcoa Highway Bridge, you can reach the **UT Medical Center**. This hospital and research center, constructed in 1952-56 with later additions, is a self-supporting facility.

To complete the walking tour, turn right on Melrose Place to the junction with Melrose Avenue. Turn left, headed west, and walk half a block to **Hopecote** at 1820 Melrose Avenue; the cottage, completed in 1924 and built in the architecture of the Cotswold District of England, is now the guest house of the university. It was originally the home of Albert G. Hope, a great-great grandson of the English builder Thomas Hope who settled in Knoxville in 1795. The two-story stucco was designed by John F. Staub, a student at the university who became a well-known architect. The inside beams of the house were salvaged from a barn on the homeplace of Admiral David Farragut. You'll also find on this street other residences built in the 1920s and now used for religious centers and fraternity houses.

Return to the beginning of Melrose Avenue and turn left on Melrose Place, which forms a loop. At the top of the loop, where Hess Hall now stands, there was once a large mansion begun in the late 1850s by John J. Craig, the founder of the Craig marble company. Before the house could be completed, the Civil War began and Craig left the South, not to return until after the war. He sold the home to Oliver Perry Temple, a lawyer and author who was also a railroad entrepreneur. Temple completed the house. His daughter was Mary Boyce Temple, who founded the Bonny Kate Chapter of the Daughters of the American Revolution in 1893 and who led the fight to save Blount Mansion in the early years. The suburban estate the house occupied was called "**Melrose**," after Melrose, Scotland, the home of Mary Boyce Temple's grandmother.

As you walk down Melrose Place, notice the parking lot on the right contained by the loop road. Between 1897 and 1920, seven homes were built on this lot in the Queen Anne, Shingle, Tudor, and Bungalow styles. Although these were architecturally significant homes, none remain.

At the junction with Lake Avenue, turn left. Along this avenue you'll enter a neighborhood of homes built in 1920-30 that has been recommended as an historic district on the National Register. The homes are a varied collection of the revival styles popular in the early 1900s. Although a few homes are still residences, most are now owned by the university and serve as offices and fraternity houses. On Lake Avenue, walk west for five blocks to 22nd Street; along the way you'll see on the left a park between 19th and Mountcastle Streets. Turn left on 22nd Street one block to Terrace Avenue and turn left. After four blocks, Terrace curves left and joins Lake Avenue. Turn right on Lake Avenue to return to Melrose Place. Cross the street and bear right to walk the other side of the loop formed by Melrose Place, and you'll find on the left the other part of Melrose Avenue beside the John C. Hodges Library. Turn left on Melrose Avenue to Volunteer Boulevard. Along the way stands the **Tyson House** on your left at 1609 Melrose. The house was designed by George Barber and built in 1907 as a residence for Lawrence D. Tyson, a prominent army officer, businessman, and U. S. Senator. Unfortunately, the Tyson House has been extensively remodeled and has been robbed of some of its grandeur by the removal of its front steps and garden walls and by the high-rise dormitories that crowd its grounds.

At Volunteer Boulevard, turn left. Notice across the street the **William B. Stokely Center for Management Studies**, completed in 1975, that is part of the College of Business Administration. On the west side of Volunteer Boulevard stand **Dunford, Greve**, and **Henson Halls**, which provide administrative support, dormitory, and academic space. Henson Hall, designed by Barber & McMurry and completed in 1931, is named for Martha C. Henson, who upon her death left money for the construction of a women's dormitory. At the time it was the largest dormitory on campus; it was converted to office space with the construction of other dormitories, such as Greve Hall in 1955, named for Harriet Greve, dean of women. Dunford Hall was built in 1963 and named for Ralph Dunford, dean of students. Greve and Dunford were also designed by Barber & McMurry.

Across the street at 1900 Volunteer Boulevard is the **Fulton Residence**, the home of Weston M. Fulton, a UT instructor who became wealthy after inventing the sylphon, a predecessor of the thermostat, and organizing a company to manufacture a variety of products using the device. The home was a gift from Fulton to the university to memorialize his son W. M. Fulton, Jr., who died in 1928. Today the home is the Student Counseling Center. Beside the Fulton home is the **Minority Student Affairs Building** that was originally a residence built in 1935. **Temple Court**, built in 1900, was originally an apartment building.

When you reach Henson Hall on the left, take the diagonal walkway that passes the front of Henson, and then turn right over the **William B. Nolan Pedestrian Bridge** that crosses Cumberland Avenue; Nolan was the first student member of the Board of Trustees and later a state legislator. Just to the left of the beginning of the pedestrian walkway stands a residence built about 1905 that is now the **School of Planning Annex**.

On the other side of Cumberland Avenue, to the left, is **Clement Hall**, a dormitory designed by Barber & McMurry and built in 1965 and named for Tennessee Governor Frank Clement, 1953-59 and 1963-67. If you were to continue west, you would cross 17th Street and enter a stretch along Cumberland Avenue lined with shops, bookstores, and restaurants called "The Strip." You'll find among the many restaurants **Sam & Andy's**, the **Copper Cellar**, and at the far end, **Old College Inn**.

Facing you at the end of the pedestrian bridge is **Sophronia Strong Hall**, named for the mother of Benjamin Rush Strong, a benefactor of the university. The first unit of this women's dormitory was completed in 1925. Later additions created a building with five wings, which are named for the first five women to attend the university, then known as Blount College. These were Barbara Blount, Polly McClung, Jenny Armstrong, Mattie Kain, and Kitty Kain. The attendance of these women at Blount College allows UT the claim of being the first coed university in the country, but in fact the presence of these women at the college was one of the exigencies of frontier life when there was no other place for women to be educated and so they were admitted to the preparatory department, the equivalent of today's high school. Women soon stopped attending the school and were not to appear as students on the university campus again until 1893.

From Strong Hall, turn east to the corner of Volunteer Boulevard; to the left is 16th Street. You'll find here an historical marker commemorating the Civil War Battle of Fort Sanders, for which the neighborhood to the north is named.

Cross 16th and walk east on Cumberland Avenue. On your left you'll see the **Panhellenic Building**, designed by Painter, Weeks, and McCarty and built in 1964, the **International House** designed by George Barber as a residence and built in 1912 that later became one of the properties of Weston M. Fulton, and the **George C. Taylor Law Center**, another Barber & McMurry design, built in 1949-50 and named for a federal district judge who was a 1908 alumnus of the College of Law. Across Cumberland on your right, you'll see **Alumni Hall**, which was originally Aconda Court Apartments but was purchased by the university in 1938 for faculty housing until it was converted for use by the Alumni Association in 1962. Next, set back from Cumberland Avenue, stands the **Carolyn P. Brown Memorial University Center**, which was designed by Barber & McMurry and constructed in 1954 from a trust set up by John Scruggs Brown in memory of his wife. The center contains offices, meeting areas, and restaurants.

At the corner, cross 15th Street, which is Stadium Drive to the right. You'll see an historical marker about James Agee, the writer who once lived in the Fort Sanders Neighborhood.

Continue east on Cumberland to complete the UT campus tour. Across Cumberland on your right, you'll see that you have returned to The Hill. At the bottom stands the **Walters Life Science Building**, constructed in 1978 and named for Herbert S. Walters, a U. S. Senator from Tennessee, 1963-64. On your left is the **James D. Hoskins Library**, designed by Barber & McMurry and built in 1931 when The Hill's Carnegie Library could no longer hold the library collection. The land on which the Hoskins Library stands is the former homesite of W. W. Woodruff, Sr., who founded Woodruff's. When the university acquired the property, the huge Woodruff Mansion was used as a women's dormitory until it was razed for the construction of the library, which was named for the university President, 1934-46. The Hoskins Library was the university's main library until the John C. Hodges Library was expanded and became the principal library. The Hoskins Library today contains the Special Collections Branch of rare books and manuscripts, the Office of the University Historian, and the Tennessee Presidential Center, containing the offices of the publications projects for editing the papers of Tennessee's three presidents: James K. Polk, Andrew Jackson, and Andrew Johnson.

Across from the Hoskins Library, you'll see The Hill entrance to the university. Continue east on Cumberland. You'll pass on your left the **Textile Materials Research Laboratory** that occupies a former residence built about 1900 and then, after crossing 13th Street, also on your left, the **Jesse W. Harris Human Ecology Building**, built in 1926 and later named for the first dean, 1957-58, of the College of Home Economics, as it was called then, and also the first woman to be dean of a UT college. At the corner of the block, you will be at 11th Street and will have completed the loop tour of the UT Campus.

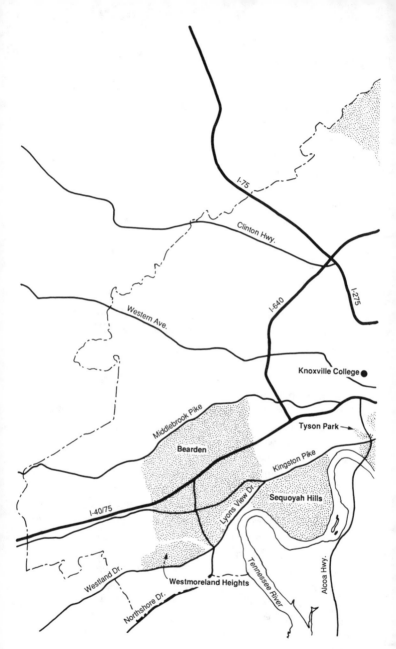

Neighborhoods

72

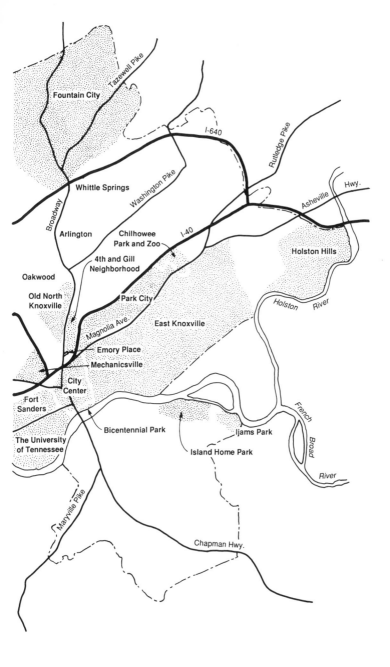

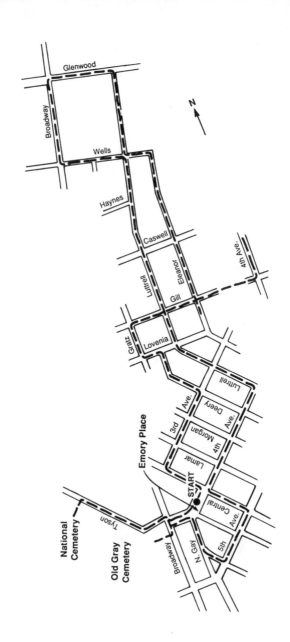

Emory Place and 4th and Gill

7 Emory Place and the 4th and Gill Neighborhood Walk

3.7 miles
Connections: Old North Knoxville Walk, Park City Tour

Attractions: This walk starts at Emory Place and Old Gray Cemetery and takes you through the 4th and Gill Neighborhood that features turn-of-the-century houses in the Victorian Cottage, Queen Anne, and Bungalow styles.

Start: Begin your walk at Emory Place, located 0.7 mile north of the city center on Broadway from the intersection of Henley Street, Western Avenue, and Summit Hill Drive. Emory Place can also be reached at the northern end of Gay Street and north on Central Street to 4th Avenue.

Description: The railroad connections before and after the Civil War propelled Knoxville to the rank of one of the leading trade centers in the south before the turn of the century. With the accompanying population growth, there was a resulting demand for housing. Aided by the coming of the streetcar that provided access to and from the city's perimeters, people were able to move to newly established suburbs to the north and west. To the north, they settled in the 4th and Gill Neighborhood and Old North Knoxville.

Both of these neighborhoods were intimately linked with the city center through the commercial district at **Emory Place** at the northern end of Gay Street. At one time there was a post office and a fire station at Emory Place in addition to various businesses that included meat markets, general stores, storage and furniture companies, a paste and polish company, a chewing gum factory, a farmers' market, and a box factory. There was also a depot, or waiting room, for the train and later the trolley line to Fountain City. At one time the plaza between the Emory Place buildings contained Emory Park, the first city park, which has since been paved over for parking.

75

Emory Place

In recent years, Emory Place has been restored in a renovation spearheaded by the architectural firms that have located their offices in the area, primarily Grieve & Ruth Architects that occupies an old commercial building at **10 Emory Place**. Another architectural firm occupies the old post office at **15 Emory Place**. The commercial buildings at Emory Place were built between 1890 and 1925 in a mixture of Victorian Vernacular, Beaux Arts, and Eastlake styles. On the southwest corner stands **St. John's Lutheran Church** at 544 Broadway, built in 1913 on the site of a marble cutting business. The church is now on the National Register of Historic Places. Emory Place has been proposed for an historic district on the National Register.

Across Broadway on the west side of Emory Place, you'll find **Old Gray Cemetery**, named for Thomas Gray who wrote, "The paths of glory lead but to the grave," in arguably the best-known poem in the English language, "An Elegy Written in a Country Churchyard" (1751). Glory indeed led to this graveyard. You'll find buried here among the statues, walkways, and marble and limestone markers many of the city's leaders in politics, education, art, and industry.

The cemetery contains twenty-six Knoxville mayors, several U.S. senators and representatives, and a Tennessee governor, William G. Brownlow. Governor Robert Taylor was also buried here before his body was moved to Johnson City. There are also judges, attorneys, and state officials. Charles McClung is interred here, the surveyor, merchant, and lawyer who laid out the lots for the City of Knoxville in 1791.

At Old Gray, you'll find William B. Reese and Thomas W. Humes who were presidents of East Tennessee University that later became the University of Tennessee. Many deans, professors, and teachers also lie here. And then there is painter and historian Russell Briscoe, impressionist painter Catherine Wiley, portrait and historical painter Lloyd Branson, historian and editor of the definitive history of Knox County (*The French Broad-Holston Country*) Mary U. Rothrock, theater-owner and mayor Peter Staub. Charles M. McGhee established Lawson McGhee Library. Calvin M. McClung, a trustee of the library, collected historical documents and books that became the basis for the

McClung Collection housed in the East Tennessee Historical Center in the city center.

The industrialists that lie in Old Gray include John J. Craig, Sr. and Jr., who were founders of a marble business. There are also J. Allen Smith of White Lily Flour, Peter Kern of Kern's Bakery, James Maynard of Brookside Mills.

As you wander through the cemetery, you'll find elaborate hand carvings, some signed by the carvers. Old Gray, established in 1850, is a private cemetery maintained by a trust fund; occasionally someone is still buried in Old Gray in family plots. To the west of the city center, there is also a New Gray Cemetery.

Adjacent to Old Gray, you'll also find the **National Cemetery** where Knoxville's soldiers are buried. A sign at the corner of Broadway and Tyson beside Old Gray points to the cemetery. National was established in 1863 during the Civil War, and you'll find in the cemetery a memorial to the Union soldiers who fought and died in the war. Tennessee supplied 31,000 men to fight on the Union side; 6000 died. The old red-brick house that served as the office of the National Cemetery, along with the wrought iron and stone fences, gateposts, monuments, and artwork of both cemeteries, has been recommended for listing on the National Register.

Before beginning your walk to the 4th and Gill Neighborhood from Emory Place, walk around the block formed by North Gay Street, 5th Avenue, and Central Street. If you have been visiting Old Gray, cross Broadway back to Emory Place and then turn right on N. Gay Street. Just before reaching 5th Avenue, bear left on Williams Street to 5th Avenue. On the left corner, stands the **First Christian Church**, built about 1920. Turn east on 5th Avenue, and just past the church you'll find old apartment buildings renovated to condominiums that are projects of Kristopher and Company. There's **Sterchi Oaks**, which was originally "Sterchi Flats" and more recently the "William Blount Hotel." The adjacent **Lucerne** was also a Sterchi family project; the Sterchis were from Lucerne, Switzerland. The condominium behind the Lucerne, **L'Hotel**, was originally the "Nina," which was the name of one of the Sterchis.

At the end of the next block, you'll also find old townhouses renovated to offices and residences, and apartments that wrap around the corner of 5th with Central. On the opposite corner, you'll see the old **Knoxville High School**, the city's largest when it opened in 1910; the school was designed by Baumann Brothers in a Colonial Revival design. It closed as a school in 1951 and became the central offices for Knoxville City Schools and continues as a school office building now that the city and county schools have merged.

From this corner, you can begin the driving tour of Park City east on 5th Avenue. To continue this walk, turn left on Central back to Emory Place. From Emory Place turn right on 4th Avenue. At Lamar Street and 4th, you'll enter the 4th Avenue and Gill Street Neighborhood.

The 4th and Gill Neighborhood was constructed in three segments. The southern section that runs north to Lovenia Avenue, called the "Staub-VanGilder-Henderson Addition," was constructed during the years 1880 to 1900. This area had already been annexed by the city in 1855. The homes in this southern section are mainly Victorian cottages and plain two-story Victorian houses.

Gill's Addition was added northward to Haynes Place during the years 1900 to 1920. The homes in this section are primarily ornate Queen Anne structures interspersed with smaller, less ornate vernacular renditions. The elaborate Queen Annes are characterized by asymmetrical composition of massed porches, turrets, balconies, and bay windows; they have steep roofs and rich exteriors with carved brackets, scrolls, pendants, and panels and porches with spindles and lattice work. The vernacular houses try for the Queen Anne style by using shingle work, turned posts, and ornamental attic vents.

Then during the years 1915 to 1930, additional homes were constructed from Haynes Place northward to about Glenwood Avenue. The homes in this section are primarily of Bungalow design, which is characterized by heavy bracketing, exposed rafter ends, tapered porch posts, and less acute roof angles with the roofs often multigabled.

These last two sections, which had become part of the incorporated town of North Knoxville, were annexed by the city in 1897. In addition to the three basic styles of architecture in 4th and Gill, there are occasional interspersed structures of Colonial

Revival, Italianate, Stick, and Gothic styles.

The three sections of the 4th and Gill Neighborhood were built to house middle and upper class workers and professionals. At one time it was considered an elite section of the city where lived doctors, lawyers, teachers, preachers, and clerical people in addition to mill and railroad workers. The textile industry was a big employer in Knoxville, and many in 4th and Gill worked in the Standard Knitting Mills to the east.

In the late 1920s and early 1930s, many people began to rent portions of their homes, and in many cases sublet, to have additional income as the economic depression of the '30s worsened. The practice continued to increase in the 1940s as rooms were made available to house people who came to the city to work in the war effort. After the war, the middle class left the neighborhood, moving to suburbs west and farther north. The stately houses and comfortable homes were steadily converted to rental units by absentee landlords. The neighborhood fell into disrepair. Adding to the deterioration, the interstate highway system was built in Knoxville in the 1960s, and I-40 virtually severed the neighborhood from the city center.

In recent years, 4th and Gill has seen a revitalization with the growing recognition of the importance of preserving historic neighborhoods. Young, educated adults have been drawn to the community by the old homes and the need for a community organization to save this important piece of Knoxville's history. The interest of these new residents has gone far in revitalizing the neighborhood. Many of the homes have been restored, and as you walk the neighborhood, you'll see the renovation work continuing. This effort has been aided by the 1985 designation of the neighborhood as an historic district on the National Register with 275 contributing structures.

Once you have entered the historic district, continue on 4th, crossing Morgan and Deery Streets to the corner of Luttrell Street, where you'll see the **4th Avenue Apartments** at 403 and 405 N. 4th Avenue. These three-story frame and brick Colonial Revival buildings were constructed about 1920.

Turn left on Luttrell. Notice a few businesses on the right that are all that is left of a commercial section of the neighborhood that spilled over from the city center along Luttrell that once connected with Depot Avenue in the Warehouse District. To the right Luttrell now deadends at the interstate.

As you proceed up Luttrell, you'll walk the section of the neighborhood that is the Staub-VanGilder-Henderson Addition. Notice the frequency of Victorian cottages constructed in 1880-1900. The occasional brick houses were built around 1920 on lots where the original houses have either burned or been torn down.

After crossing 3rd Avenue, you'll see on your left at **703 Luttrell** a George Barber cottage built in the Queen Anne style in 1890. Barber was the well-known architect of mail-order houses and house plans and many Knoxville residences.

Continue on Luttrell to the intersection of Luttrell and Lovenia. On the left, you'll see at **416 Lovenia** a Gothic Revival church listed on the National Register that was constructed around 1910 as the Trinity Methodist Church. The congregation moved from this area in the 1960s, and today the structure is occupied by the Knoxville House of Faith. Diagonally across the intersection on the right, stands a Tudor Revival church at **800 Luttrell**. Constructed around 1900, the building was the Luttrell Street Methodist Church; the church was also once the Seventh Day Adventist Church, and today it contains Brooks Photography.

From Lovenia Avenue, continue on Luttrell which bears to the right into Gill's Addition. For the next three blocks, as you cross Gill Avenue and Caswell Place to Haynes Place, you'll see several beautifully restored homes. At **806-814 Luttrell** notice four restored cottages built about 1900 in a simple Queen Anne style some call "Princess Anne." J. G. Sterchi lived in the house at **820 Luttrell**. Sterchi with his brothers founded Sterchi Brothers Furniture. He later acquired sole interest in the company and turned it into a chain of stores throughout the south.

At **901-903 Luttrell** stands another recent residential renovation of Kristopher and Company. Then at **907 Luttrell** is another George Barber House, a two-story Victorian Vernacular built in 1895. At 911 Luttrell stands the **Sullivan House**, a two-story Queen Anne built in 1900 that is thought to be the home of Michael Sullivan, the son of Patrick Sullivan, who operated Sullivan's Saloon in the city center. Notice the iron hoops embedded in the curb in front of the Sullivan House, maybe for tying horses. Then at 927 Luttrell is the **Scharringhaus House**, the residence of Edward H. Scharringhaus who was involved in the Appalachian Exposition held in Knoxville in 1910 and who was director of the National Conservation Exhibition held in Knoxville in 1913. Notice also the nicely restored 1900 Queen Anne at **933 Luttrell**.

After crossing Caswell, you'll see on the northwest corner at **1003 Luttrell** a large Queen Anne built about 1900 that recently burned. At 1007 Luttrell stands the **1889 House**, a Victorian Vernacular with Gothic influences. At **1018 Luttrell** is a nicely remodeled Colonial Revival built about 1910. At **1019** and **1021 Luttrell** are restored 1905 Vernacular homes.

At Haynes Place, continue north on Luttrell into the third section of the neighborhood. There is some overlap here in styles, but you'll notice you eventually leave the large two-story Queen Annes and see more of the Bungalow houses.

At Wells Avenue, turn left headed west to Broadway. At the southeast corner of Wells and Gratz Street at **800-802 Wells**, notice the large Colonial Revival with wooden columns built about 1905. At Broadway, turn right.

At 1306 N. Broadway, you'll walk in front of **Greystone**, a house built in the Richardson Romanesque style for Major Eldad Cicero Camp in 1890, and so also called the "Camp House." Camp was a Union major during the Civil War who later came to Knoxville. He made a fortune in coal and marble and was also a lawyer and U. S. Attorney. His residence, designed by Alfred B. Mullett, who also designed the Custom House in the city center, is on the National Register. The house now contains the TV stations of WATE. Notice the carriage house to the right in back, and at the house itself notice the stained glass above the doors and windows.

At the corner of Glenwood Avenue, turn right headed east on Glenwood to reenter the 4th and Gill Neighborhood. At this corner, you can also cross Broadway to the left to connect with the Old North Knoxville Neighborhood Walk.

Along Glenwood, headed east, you'll pass the **Brownlow Elementary School** on your right. At the corner of Glenwood and Luttrell, turn south on Luttrell to Wells Avenue; again watch for the Bungalow style houses.

1018 Luttrell Street (David Cann)

At Wells Avenue, turn left one block to Eleanor Street and then right on Eleanor. At the corner at **1127 Eleanor** on your right stands a home in the American four square style built about 1915. You'll pass through one long block back into Gill's Addition to Caswell Place (Haynes Place does not penetrate this block). Along the way at **1024 Eleanor** on your left you'll see a 1905 Queen Anne cottage with beveled glass transom and sidelights. At **1015**, **1019**, and **1023 Eleanor** on your right stand three restored two-story Victorian Vernacular homes built about 1900.

Then at 1003 Eleanor is a Colonial Revival built about 1900 with Ionic columns and recessed transom thought to be the **Kluttz Home**; Kluttz was at one time the partner of architect George Barber. At the northeast corner of Eleanor and Caswell, notice the brass street names embedded in the concrete curb. Cross Caswell. On the southwest corner of Caswell and Eleanor, on the right, is a nicely remodeled Colonial Revival at **941 Eleanor** built about 1905. Then on your left at **932 Eleanor** is a large Colonial Revival in good condition with large wooden columns, built about 1900.

Continue south on Eleanor to Gill Avenue. Turn left on Gill and cross under the interstate to the corner of 4th and Gill, you'll find the **4th and Gill Neighborhood Center** at 800 N. 4th Avenue. The center occupies a two-story Victorian Vernacular house built around 1885. Because of the center's location, the neighborhood has become known as "4th and Gill." Across from the neighborhood center once stood the mansion of Alfred Taylor, governor of Tennessee 1920-22; the elaborate two-story Queen Anne house built in 1880 and listed on the National Register burned in the mid-1980s. Alfred Taylor was the brother of Governor Robert Taylor who was buried for a time in Old Gray. The brothers ran for governor against each other in the election of 1886, which was termed the "War of the Roses" because they were known as "The Knights of the Roses." The title had originated from an off-the-cuff remark by Robert that although they were like roses from the same garden, Alf was a scarlet rose, while he was a rose of pure white. Robert Taylor won the election and served two terms. Alf Taylor was later elected governor.

To the north on 4th Avenue, notice the elaborate eave decoration on the 1880 Victorian house at **812 4th Avenue**; the decorative pattern includes Xs, Hs, Os, and math symbols. You'll find a finely restored George Barber house at **816**, a Queen Anne built in the 1880s. At **820 4th Avenue** is a restored Queen Anne built in 1885 in which a restaurant is expected to open.

After exploring this section of the neighborhood, return to the corner of Eleanor and Gill. You can also explore into the next block south on Eleanor where you'll find a small neighborhood park and at **817 Eleanor** an elaborate Queen Anne house built about 1895. But to continue the tour, walk west on Gill Avenue. Cross Luttrell Street and turn left on Gratz Street.

At the corner of Lovenia Avenue and Gratz, you'll see the old **McCallie School** on the west side of Gratz, built in 1907. J. H. McCallie was superintendent of schools.

Turn left on Lovenia to Deery Street. On the left, you'll see Italianate apartment buildings constructed around 1900 at **415-417 Lovenia**. Notice the white frame Colonial Revival cottage on your right that was the **Lovenia Baumann House**, at 839 Deery Street. This was a home built for the younger brothers and sisters of Joseph Baumann of the well-known Baumann Brothers architectural firm. One of the sisters' names was "Lovenia," which also became the name of the avenue. At the northwest corner of Lovenia and Deery, in front of the house, you can find more of the old brass street names embedded in the curb.

Turn right on Deery, which bears to the left to 3rd Avenue. Turn right on 3rd to Morgan Street. On the southeast corner of Morgan and 3rd, you'll see a Bungalow style house and next to it **Cleveland Park on Morgan** at 729, a nicely preserved three-story apartment house built in 1925; the restoration was another Kristopher and Company project. Continue on 3rd across Morgan, and in the next block on the right stands **Central United Methodist Church**, a Gothic Revival built in 1926.

Continue on 3rd Avenue, and cross Lamar Street to Central Street. Turn left to return to Emory Place.

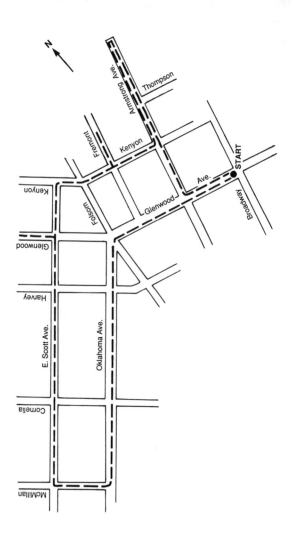

N

START

Armstrong Ave.

Thompson

Fremont

Kenyon

Kenyon

Folsom

Glenwood

Ave.

Glenwood

Broadway

Harvey

E. Scott Ave.

Oklahoma Ave.

Cornelia

McMillan

Old North Knoxville

86

⑧ Old North Knoxville Walk

2 miles
Connections: 4th and Gill Neighborhood Walk; Oakwood,
Arlington, and Whittle Springs Tour

Attractions: This walk takes you through the Old North
Knoxville neighborhood of finely restored Queen Anne and Neoclassical homes that was once part of North Knoxville.

Start: Begin at the corner of Glenwood Avenue and Broadway,
1.5 miles north on Broadway from the intersection of Henley
Street, Western Avenue, and Summit Hill Drive in the city center.

Description: Many people were attracted to the commercial and
industrial growth in Knoxville during the latter 1800s. There was
an obvious demand for housing that accompanied this growth,
and so residential districts spread to the north and west. It was
natural that much of this development occurred along Broadway,
which led to unincorporated Fountain City; in 1886 Broadway
was the widest street in Knoxville, which is probably one of the
reasons it was given that name.

Like the 4th and Gill Neighborhood east of Broadway, the
neighborhood of Old North Knoxville west of Broadway spread
by several additions: the large Mountain View Addition and the
Galbraith and Kerns Addition northward, and east of these,
smaller additions that included Anderson, Dameron, and Shep-
ards. The community of North Knoxville began to take shape in
the late 1800s as the additions were subdivided, lots sold, and
homes constructed. The community incorporated as the City of
North Knoxville in 1889 but was annexed by Knoxville in 1897.

The neighborhood that is now called "Old North Knoxville"
is bounded by Broadway, Central Street, and Woodland Avenue,
which form a triangle pointing northeast; some of it contains
commercial establishments and a few residences built in the last
few decades. The original homes that remain in the community,
built from about 1890 to 1925, are large Queen Anne and

Neoclassical houses and smaller cottages along the ridge that runs north through the community; small laborers' homes sit at the base on either side of the ridge.

The houses along the ridge crest were the homes of professionals, industrialists, and managers in Knoxville's businesses and industries. Many were associated with the Southern Railroad, which had its terminal and office not far to the south, and Brookside Cotton Mills, which in 1902 was the largest employer in the city at its location on Baxter Avenue to the southwest.

With the coming of the Great Depression, most houses were divided into multifamily dwellings, rented, or left vacant. After the depression and World War II, the young middle class settled in the newer subdivisions that were growing west and farther north of Knoxville. The North Knoxville neighborhood continued to gradually deteriorate in a similar pattern of absentee landlords and transient renters that eviscerated the 4th and Gill Neighborhood. Some homes that stayed in good shape were those in which the families of original owners held out against the encroaching deterioration or were those that otherwise remained single-family dwellings.

Then in the late 1970s, a revitalization effort began to save the neighborhood, which has been determined to be eligible for the National Register of Historic Places. Young professionals moved into the community, attracted to the grand old houses that needed saving. On your walk through the neighborhood, you'll see finely restored homes and much renovation work being carried out.

Begin at the corner of Glenwood Avenue and Broadway. From this corner you can also connect with the 4th and Gill Neighborhood on the other side of Broadway by walking east on Glenwood.

Notice the **Fourth Presbyterian Church** on the southwest corner. The congregation formed in 1886, and the original church was on the site of the Brownlow School in 4th and Gill. The present Gothic Revival building was erected in 1913.

Walk west on Glenwood to Armstrong Avenue and turn right into one of the more affluent sections of the old neighborhood. At the southwest corner of Armstrong and Kenyon Street, notice the Victorian house at **1329 Armstrong** that has a diagonal sidewalk leading from the entrance to the corner. You'll notice several of the corner houses on this tour have this diagonal walkway.

As you cross Kenyon Street, you'll see that the street is concrete, notched in a brick pattern to provide better traction. You'll find embedded in the intersection a plate bearing the name of the company that constructed the street. Many streets in Knoxville were once made this way. All but a few have been paved over with asphalt. Also notice at the northeast corner of the intersection the brass street names embedded in the sidewalk curb, a practice that was also common in 4th & Gill.

After crossing Kenyon Street, Armstrong stretches for one more block where you'll find several large homes. Notice the third-floor window in the house on the left at **1345 Armstrong** that offers a view southeast to the Great Smoky Mountains, part of the southern Appalachian Mountains southeast of Knoxville. Many of the houses in Old North Knoxville have windows high on the southeast side to take advantage of this view to the mountains, which is presumably how the Mountain View Addition got its name.

At **1355 Armstrong**, you'll see a large well-maintained Tudor Revival. On the right at the corner of Armstrong and Thompson Place, at **1001 Thompson**, stands a fully renovated Queen Anne house originally constructed in 1898. To the left of the house on the Armstrong side, you'll see the original carriage house that went with the residence. Many of the large homes had barns and carriage houses for maintaining horses and carriages in the early years.

Then at **1361 Armstrong**, you'll find a Neoclassical residence with Italianate influence constructed about 1925; at **1365**, a Shingle style residence; at **1402**, a brick cottage; at **1405**, an apartment house that was originally a residence; at **1408**, a Colonial Revival cottage built about 1920; and at **1411**, a Neoclassical residence built around 1900 that is now the meeting place of a professional women's sorority.

Armstrong Avenue ends in a cul-de-sac at the **Dunn House** at 1424 Armstrong, a large residence with Corinthian columns built in 1906 for J. M. Dunn. Notice the carriage house on the left.

1001 Thompson Place (David Cann)

In addition to the carriage houses, barns, and other outbuildings to house and care for a horse and carriage, and occasional milk cows and chickens, most homes also had cisterns that served as a water source until city water was extended into the neighborhood around 1910.

From the Dunn House, retrace your steps to Kenyon Street and turn west up the hill. At **1111 Kenyon**, you'll see a 1909 cottage. At **1120** and **1122 Kenyon** are two houses built in 1904. At the northwest corner of Kenyon and Fremont stands a stucco and timber Tudor Revival-style Bungalow at 1200 Kenyon that was the **Cruze House**, built in 1914 as the home of Christopher Cruze, vice president of Wright Cruze Hardware Co.; the front door has the original hinges and hardware. On the southeast corner, at **1428 Fremont**, you'll find a fine brick Bungalow with heavy columns.

Before continuing up Kenyon, turn right, headed north on Fremont, to **1523 Fremont**, on the left. The cluster of different windows on the northeast side of the house is unique. On the right along Fremont, you'll find you are at the back of the large homes on Armstrong Avenue. Farther down the street, Freemont once led into a community called "Muck Town" that reputedly housed blacks who worked as servants in the big homes on the hill; they could have walked up the hill on Freemont from their homes and entered the backs of the large houses on Armstrong.

Return to Kenyon Street and continue uphill on Kenyon to Folsom Avenue. Look to the left on Folsom to see large chimney pots on the first house on the left. In the next block on Kenyon beyond Folsom are the **Stegall Houses**. E.H. Stegall and his wife, Amanda, lived at 1300 Kenyon, built about 1912. Stegall was vice president of Cherokee Coal Co., but he and his wife also must have dabbled in real estate development because they also owned at one time the houses at 1301 built in 1924 and at 1303, 1307, and 1311 built around 1926.

At East Scott Avenue, turn left. Toward the end of the block on the left, you'll find a Bungalow at **708 E. Scott** that has Oriental influence; the home was originally built for a woman physician and missionary to China. At **704 E. Scott**, notice the wrought iron fence in front of the 1912 clapboard house. At **707** on the right, you'll find a Victorian built about 1895. At the corner with Glenwood, notice a large Bungalow style house on the left at **700 E. Scott** and, on the right, a Queen Anne cottage with Eastlake influences at **701** that has not been altered much since it was built about 1893.

The walking tour continues straight on E. Scott Avenue from Glenwood. But first turn right down Glenwood for a short distance to a notable cottage on the left at **518 Glenwood**. It is French Eclectic in style with slate roof and smooth stucco exterior. The cottage was designed by David West Barber, who lived there; Barber was a cousin of Charles Barber of Barber & McMurry and was also a member of the architectural firm. From here the Oakwood, Arlington, and Whittle Springs Tour continues down Glenwood. To continue the Old North Knoxville walk, turn around and walk back up Glenwood.

At the corner of E. Scott and Glenwood, turn right on Scott. The first house on the left is the **Newman House** at 522 E. Scott. The residence was originally designed by Barber and Kluttz and built in 1892 in the Queen Anne style, but the house burned and was rebuilt in the Neoclassical style in the early 1900s. The house was first occupied by S. B. and Rena Newman; Newman founded the S. B. Newman Printing Co., which still operates in Knoxville.

The **Anderson House** at 523 Scott, on the right, was built by Henry Anderson for himself and his wife, Mary, about 1923. The house was designed by West Barber who lived on Glenwood.

At **516 E. Scott**, you'll see a home built for Karl and Agnes Baum about 1919. Baum was secretary and treasurer of Baum's Florist, which operated in Knoxville until a few years ago. At **517 E. Scott**, stands a Neoclassical home with large porch columns built in 1912 for B. B. Bayler, a traveling salesman.

The Victorian cottage at **510 E. Scott** was built about 1906 for E. M. and Mary Sweetman; he was an engineer for the Southern Railroad. The southern colonial at **509 Scott** was built about the same time for Vernon C. and Halie Tindell; Tindell was secretary of the Merchants Protective Association.

The Neoclassical home at **502 E. Scott** was built in 1906 for H. A. E. and Mary Parsons; he was a bookkeeper for a grocery located on Market Square and later secretary and treasurer of W. W. Woodruff Hardware Co. that was located in Knoxville's city center and which still operates there as Woodruff's.

518 Glenwood Avenue (David Cann)

At 505 E. Scott you'll see the **Getaz Home**, a Queen Anne built by David Getaz for himself and his wife, Maggie, in 1889. Getaz was a Swiss immigrant who with C. T. Stephenson, an Englishman, formed the building and architect firm of Stephenson & Getaz that in 1885 built the old Knox County Courthouse in Knoxville's city center. Some say that Getaz went bankrupt building his home; he was removed from the Stephenson & Getaz firm for a time. A later occupant of the home in 1907-14 was W. H. Sterchi, one of the original founders of Sterchi Brothers Furniture. If you walk around the corner on Harvey Street, you'll see the original carriage house and barn behind the old mansion.

Continue down E. Scott. In the next block, at **417 E. Scott**, notice the leaded glass in the doors and windows of this house built in 1892 as the home of a physician, Dr. C. M. Cawood. At **411**, you'll find a 1909 residence that has been extensively remodeled; it was the home of Abe M. Baughman, an engineer for the Southern Railroad.

Cross Cornelia Street. On the corner at **240 E. Scott** is a Neoclassical home built in 1904 for Charles W. Kinzel, a carpenter for the Southern Railroad. You'll see a nicely restored Queen Anne at **241 E. Scott**, built in 1896 for James Fair who founded Fair Iron Foundry that made cast iron and steel ranges. At **235** you'll find a brick Bungalow and, at **232**, a Victorian Vernacular built in 1902 for the Buchanan family; Buchanan was a machine shop foreman for the Southern Railroad. In the remainder of the block you'll see several homes in the Neoclassical style.

Cross McMillan Street; notice the brass street names in the curb. On your right at 131 E. Scott stands **Pine Crest**, a George Barber home built in 1900 for W. T. Lang, an official at Brookside Mills. Notice the stained glass in the chimney. This block between McMillan and Central was part of the McMillan estate where once the McMillan House stood on Central.

At this corner of Scott and McMillan, turn left on McMillan. At the next corner turn left on Oklahoma Avenue. As you walk along the tree-shaded street, you'll cross Cornelia and Harvey. At **201** and **215 Oklahoma**, you'll find two Victorian homes with Shingle influences. At **237** is a Victorian cottage. The house at **505** is a Shingle cottage; then at **517** is a brick home in the Federal style. At the corner of Oklahoma and Glenwood stands an

94

Eastlake-style house at **523 Oklahoma** built around 1889. Notice the original brick sidewalk in front of this house and the diagonal sidewalk from the house to the corner.

At this junction of Oklahoma, Glenwood, and Folsom, bear right on Glenwood Avenue. Farther to the right on Folsom and then on Anderson Avenue are some of the smaller worker homes, including several shotgun houses. In the early part of the century, that section of the neighborhood was separated by economic class from the rest of North Knoxville.

On Glenwood, **311** on the left, is a large house built sometime before 1893 but altered considerably. At **307 Glenwood** stands a large Neoclassical home built about 1900 with a rare double chimney and a widow's walk that offers a view of the mountains to the southeast. You'll see large Bungalows at **226** and **220 Glenwood** on the right. At Freemont Avenue, you can see north to an old Victorian that is now an apartment house at **1415 Freemont**.

Continue on Glenwood, and on the left at **219 Glenwood** you'll find a Neoclassical residence and, at **215**, a home with Italianate influence; notice the fan design in glass over the front door. At **212** on the right is a Tudor Revival cottage, and at **206**, a stucco home.

At **203 Glenwood**, on the northwest corner of Glenwood and Armstrong Avenue, is a yellow-brick, brown-shingled house with Neoclassical columns. Around the side on Armstrong, notice the fish pond in the backyard, not original but representative of the small ponds that were in back of many of the old homes. The ponds were primarily for ornamentation, but it is thought that fish for eating were also occasionally kept in the backyard pools.

From Armstrong, continue down Glenwood to return to Broadway.

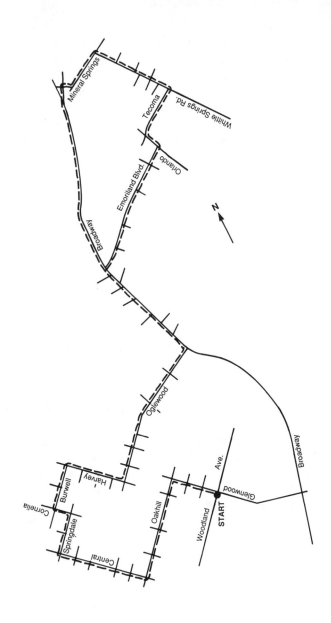

Oakwood, Arlington, and Whittle Springs

⑨ Oakwood, Arlington, and Whittle Springs Tour

6.5 miles
Connections: Old North Knoxville Walk, Fountain City Tour

Attractions: This tour passes through the neighborhoods of Oakwood and Arlington and by the Whittle Springs Hotel site.

Start: Because much of this tour is along the busy thoroughfare of Broadway, you should make this an auto excursion. Begin on Glenwood Avenue in Old North Knoxville, and head north across Woodland Avenue into Oakwood.

Description: Knoxville's suburbs continued to expand northward, gradually connecting the city with the unincorporated Fountain City area. North of North Knoxville, the community of Oakwood took shape as a developed subdivision. In 1902 the area was a forest of large oaks and pines, which is presumably how it got the name "Oakwood." By 1905, there were about 200 houses in the neighborhood. The community incorporated in 1913 as the City of Oakwood but was annexed by Knoxville in 1917. The neighborhood was served by the steam railway and later the streetcar that ran from the northern end of Knoxville's city center to Fountain City through Lincoln Park adjacent to Oakwood. From Lincoln Park, the train passed through Arlington and Whittle Springs before reaching Fountain City.

After crossing Woodland, you'll reach Oakhill Avenue in three blocks. Turn left. In the Oakwood Community, you'll find homes built in the early 1900s in the Bungalow, Neoclassical, and Victorian Vernacular styles. At the end of Oakhill in 0.4 mile, you'll emerge on Central Street. Turn right five blocks in 0.4 mile to Springdale Avenue and turn right. In two blocks at Cornelia Avenue, turn left to Burwell Avenue. Turn right on Burwell where you'll find on the right the **Oakwood Methodist Church**, built in the early 1900s.

At the end of Burwell in two blocks, turn right on Harvey Street four blocks to Oglewood Avenue. Turn left to Broadway. On your left you'll pass the **Christenberry Middle School**.

When Oglewood meets Broadway, you'll see Stevens Mortuary on the right at 1304 Oglewood. The mortuary, with additions, occupies the **Ledgerwood-Scott House**, originally the home of Col. Joseph Scott, built in 1833. The house contained hand-painted wallpaper that had originally been brought from Paris to be used in Andrew Jackson's Hermitage near Nashville. Scott purchased the wallpaper at an auction. When the Scott House became a church in 1946, before becoming a mortuary, the wallpaper was saved and placed in the dining room of the home called "Crescent Bend" on Kingston Pike.

Turn left on Broadway into the Arlington section of Knoxville. Don't miss in 0.2 mile the **La Reve House** at 2921 Broadway on your left. A Neoclassical Revival with Bungalow influences built in 1907-10, the house was designed by Charles Hayes for his brother Lynn Hayes. The La Reve House with its elaborate detailing has been recommended for the National Register. On your right in another 0.2 mile, notice the **Kentshire Apartments**, originally "Broadway Courts," built about 1928.

Soon after the apartments, turn right on Emoriland Boulevard. You'll find homes built in the 1920s and 1930s, a mix of styles including Bungalow, Tudor Revival, and Italianate. You'll also pass the old **McCampbell School** on the left.

At the end of Emoriland, turn left on Orlando Street, and then right on Tecoma Drive to Whittle Springs Road. Turn left toward Whittle Springs where there was once the large Whittle Springs Hotel that catered to guests year-round. The hotel had a spring-fed swimming pool and an 18-hole golf course that is today a city-owned golf course. In 0.3 mile, you'll pass on your right the site of the old stucco-brick hotel where the **WNOX Radio Station** now has its offices. For a time the station operated out of the old hotel, but a new building was constructed and the hotel was torn down in the 1960s.

Soon after the hotel site, you'll reach Mineral Springs Avenue; turn left 0.2 mile to Broadway. You can then turn right to reach the beginning of the Fountain City Tour, or you can turn left to get back to Glenwood Avenue and the city center.

La Reve House

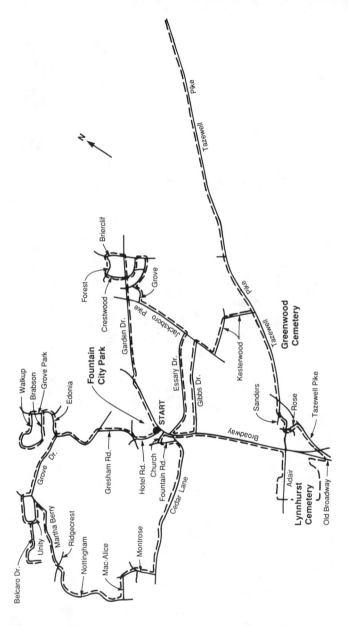

Fountain City

10 Fountain City Tour

17 miles
Connections: Oakwood, Arlington, and Whittle Springs Tour

Attractions: This tour takes you by Fountain City Park and Lake and some of the older homes of this once unincorporated community.

Start: From the intersection of Henley Street, Western Avenue, and Summit Hill Drive, head north on Broadway 5.2 miles to the corner of Hotel Road and Broadway in Fountain City, which is also 1.6 miles north from Mineral Springs Avenue on the Oakwood, Arlington, and Whittle Springs Tour.

Description: When John Adair first came to the valley between Sharp's Ridge on the south and Black Oak Ridge on the north, he saw a broad expanse of tall grass as high as a person's head. Appropriately, the area became known as "Grassy Valley."

At about the same time that James White was establishing his fort in the 1780s in what was to become the City of Knoxville, John Adair settled in Grassy Valley about six miles north of White's Fort. He claimed lands granted to him by North Carolina for his services as a collector of fees from pioneers settling in the region. It was during that period that Adair assumed responsibility for the public funds he was collecting and turned over $13,000 to John Sevier for supplies, guns, and ammunition so Sevier could engage in the Battle of King's Mountain, which proved to be a turning point in the Revolutionary War.

Because of the times, Adair also constructed a fort around his settlement. The fort came to serve as a supply depot for the Cumberland Guard, a militia that escorted settlers west across the Cumberland Plateau to the Cumberland River settlements near present-day Nashville.

Although Adair lived at a distance from the growing capital of the Southwest Territory, he participated in important activities at Knoxville. He was appointed by Governor Blount as a justice of the peace for Knox County; he was a member of the first board of trustees of Blount College and a member of the first constitutional convention for the emerging State of Tennessee. He was also one of the founding members of the First Presbyterian Church in Knoxville.

The area Adair had settled in, and to which other settlers were attracted, became known as "Fountain Head" because of the several natural springs in the valley. When a post office was opened for the first time in 1890, the name was changed to "Fountain City" to avoid confusion with another Fountain Head that was in Sumner County, Tennessee. With the addition of several neighborhoods in the intervening years and the development of a commercial district along Broadway, Fountain City grew to become one of the largest unincorporated communities in the country. It was annexed by the City of Knoxville in 1962.

To begin the tour, turn left off Broadway, headed west on Hotel Road. This area is called "The Station" because it was the northern end of the rail and streetcar line that led from Knoxville to Fountain City. The buildings along Hotel were constructed in the early 1900s. You'll pass on the right **Fountain City Park**. In the park you'll find **Fountain Head Spring**.

The park was an active area during the early 1800s, a time when camp meetings were popular. Religious services were held under big tents in the park. It was also a popular place for picnics and other gatherings and meetings. Robert and Alf Taylor debated here at a political meeting in 1886 during their "War of the Roses" campaign for the governorship.

The Fountain Head Campground lost prominence in the mid-1800s when a National Camp meeting ground was established three miles to the southwest by a Rev. Inskip; the new campground became more popular because it was near a new railroad line. The community that grew up around that campground is today known as "Inskip."

In 1885 the Fountain Head Campground was sold to the Fountain Head Improvement Company, which built a resort that included the park and a new inn, the Fountain Head Hotel. The hotel was designed by Stephenson & Getaz, the same firm that built the old Knox County Courthouse in Knoxville's City Center. A hack line brought guests to the resort from the end of the horse-drawn streetcar line in Knoxville. In 1890, a syndicate of capitalists, calling itself the "Knoxville and Fountain City Land Company," purchased 430 acres, including the hotel and park to develop a new town; Fountain City at the time still had only a few residences among mostly farmland. To provide access to the new development, a railroad line was constructed from Knoxville to Fountain City. Passengers boarded the train at Emory Place on the northern end of Knoxville for their trip to Fountain City. The train was eventually replaced with a streetcar in 1905.

After a few successful years in which the resort was popular and many residential lots were sold, the development project declined. The Fountain City Hotel passed through several owners, finally becoming a sanitarium until it burned in 1920. Later development that threatened the continued existence of the park was stopped by a lawsuit brought to the courts by the citizens of Fountain City. The suit went all the way to the State Supreme Court, which denied the developers' rights to the park land and transferred the guardianship of the park to the citizens of Fountain City. Today the park is maintained by the Fountain City Lions Club.

Continuing west on Hotel from the park, you'll see on your right at 213 Hotel the **Fountain City Branch** of the county public library system. Across from the library, stands the **Fountain City United Methodist Church** at 212 Hotel, originally the Fountain Head Methodist; the church was the principal user of the park for camp meetings in the early years.

In 0.2 mile from the beginning of Hotel Road, at the corner of Holbrook, notice the **First Baptist Church** with its projecting roof angles. Beside it to the south is the more sedate predecessor sanctuary built in 1945. Bear right, still on Hotel. On your right you'll see the **Fountain City Presbyterian Church** at 500 Hotel Road and beside it, **McCorkle Chapel**, named for a former pastor and built in 1928-29.

At the church, bear left on Gresham Road 0.1 mile to the **Gresham Middle School** on your left. This is the old Central High School and the site of Holbrook College. When the Knoxville and Fountain City Land Company began its development of a town, the company encouraged the establishment of a college, which they reasoned would provide a boost to the development of a residential district. The Fountain City branch of Holbrook College was established in 1893. Several campus buildings were constructed. The old hotel was used as a women's dormitory. The school was not very successful and was purchased by the Tennessee Baptist Association in 1900. In 1906 the county acquired the property, and Central High School operated out of the old college buildings until they were razed to make way for the present building, which has a newer addition on the left. When Central High moved to new buildings on the east side of Broadway, the old building became Gresham Middle School, named for Hassie K. Gresham, a respected educator, principal of Central High 1919-1947, and former student of Holbrook College.

At the corner of Gresham and Grove Drive, turn left and begin an ascent of Black Oak Ridge. Stay with Grove Drive 0.3 mile and turn right on Edonia Drive. In 0.2 mile, bear left on Grove Park Drive, and then in another 0.1 mile turn left on Brabson Drive. In 0.3 mile, you'll circle the **McClung House**, a large white house commanding an impressive view of Fountain City below. The house, built in 1902 for Charles J. McClung, is at 2910 Walkup Drive; the Walkup family were later owners.

Continue around the mansion on what is now Walkup Drive. After bearing to the left, you'll see a large brick home on your left at **2945 Walkup** that dates from about 1900. When Walkup Drive runs into Grove Park Drive, turn right and you'll be back at Grove Drive in 0.3 mile. Turn right on Grove and continue to Belcaro Drive on your left in 0.4 mile. You'll see at Belcaro Drive the brick entrance gate that once marked the drive to the **Belcaro Mansion**. Turn left on Belcaro Drive, which soon curves to the left and then turns right down a tree-shaded lane. At the end of the lane is Belcaro at 2000 Belcaro Drive, once the home of Hugh Lawson McClung. Hugh McClung, grandson of Charles McClung and great-grandson of James White, was a lawyer and at one time a special justice in the Supreme Court of Tennessee. The magnificent mansion, built in 1922 and recommended for listing on the National Register of Historic Places, has unfortunately been encroached upon by the surrounding neighborhood of newer homes.

104

Continue on Belcaro Drive to the right; you'll come to a deadend in 0.2 mile with room to turn around. Then return along Belcaro 0.3 mile to Unity Drive to the right, which runs into Martha Berry Drive. Turn right on Martha Berry, which in 0.4 mile runs into Ridgecrest. Turn right on Ridgecrest and then take an immediate left on Nottingham, which eventually becomes Lynnette Drive. In 0.6 mile from the beginning of Nottingham, turn left on Mac-Alice Drive and then right on Hamlet Road. Hamlet joins Montrose Road, which passes in front of **St. Joseph's School** and runs into Cedar Lane, which has a few cedar trees remaining from those that once lined both sides of the lane. Turn left on Cedar Lane, and watch for the third house on the left, at 1909 Cedar Lane, the **Karnes House**, built with Italianate detailing for James M. Karnes about 1891.

In 0.8 mile along Cedar Lane, turn left on Fountain Road. At the corner you'll see up the hill on your left, at 5301 Fountain Road, the **Gentry-Griffey Funeral Chapel**, which occupies a residence built around 1890 that overlooks **Fountain City Lake** on your right. The heart-shaped lake was part of the 1890 development of the Knoxville and Fountain City Land Company. The spring-fed lake with a fountain in the center is today the central attraction of the community. The house that is now a mortuary was built for the son of Col. J. C. Woodward, who was the head of the Knoxville and Fountain City Land Company.

At the next corner, turn right on Church Street to Broadway and turn right, headed south. In 0.2 mile, you'll pass on the right the Target Department Store that occupies the site of the home Woodward constructed for himself. The grand mansion was called "Park Place." Plans to raze the house for the department store resulted in a great public outcry, but today the house is gone.

As you continue south on Broadway, notice in half a mile on the right near the Dairy Queen the historical sign and the small stone marker under a U.S. flag that designates the approximate location of John Adair's Fort. Then in another 0.1 mile, turn right on Adair Drive. In 0.1 mile turn right into **Lynnhurst Cemetery**. Established in 1922, the cemetery occupies land that was once part of the John Adair tract. On your left, you'll see stairs that lead up a knoll to a large tree, under which you'll find an erect stone that designates the burial site of Adair.

Fountain City Lake

Stay on the cemetery road to the second left turn. Making the turn, you'll cross Adair Road and enter the south section of the cemetery. Pass all the way through the cemetery to the far side and turn left. In 0.1 mile, you'll see on your right a pond and dam that was constructed in 1923. Continue straight and you'll emerge from the cemetery on Old Broadway.

From the entrance to Lynnhurst, turn right one block to Tazewell Pike on the left. Turn left on Tazewell, which was one of the early turnpikes leading out of Knoxville; it is still a main thoroughfare, and you'll find that during the traffic rush hour you won't be able to drive as slowly as you would like.

Soon after passing under Broadway, you'll enter the Smithwood Community. Smithwood is perhaps best known for being the home of Baum's Home of Flowers, which once had 20 greenhouses in the community and more at its farm in Bearden in the west end of Knoxville. Baum's was started in 1889 by Charles L. Baum and grew to be one of the largest florist businesses in the Southeast. The business remained in operation for nearly a hundred years.

In 0.4 mile from the beginning of Tazewell Pike, turn left on Rose Drive and then bear right to Adair Drive. You will have entered **Adair Gardens**, a neighborhood of small brick homes built in the 1920s and early 1930s. Turn right on Adair, and then right on Sanders Pike to get back to Tazewell Pike. At the street light, Tazewell Pike proceeds straight ahead from Sanders.

As you continue out Tazewell Pike, you'll pass in 0.1 mile at 3203 Tazewell the old **Smithwood School**, built in 1915. It now houses the Smithwood Learning Center and the Tennessee Institute of Electronics.

In another 0.3 mile, you'll pass **Greenwood Cemetery** on your right, established in 1900; a tall monument at the back of the cemetery was erected for the son of Dr. R. M. Kesterson, who founded the cemetery. Across from the cemetery at **3601 Tazewell Pike**, you'll see the first of several houses that form a small district of Victorian homes built in the late 1800s; this one in 1890.

In 0.3 mile farther, at **4003 Tazewell Pike** on the left, you'll see an 1889 Victorian with elaborate eave decorations using X01-H-1X0X1, very similar to the decoration on the Victorian at

John Adair Gravesite

812 4th Avenue in the 4th and Gill Neighborhood. In another 0.2 mile, at 4105 Tazewell on the left, is an 1885 Victorian called "**The Oaks**." The house with the gambrel roof next to it at **4107 Tazewell** was built about 1930. In 0.1 mile farther, at 4115 Tazewell, you'll find the **Crawford House**, built by William Crawford in 1857. The Crawford House supposedly served as the Civil War headquarters for General Armstrong of Alabama in 1863. Both the Oaks and the Crawford House are eligible for the National Register.

In another 0.1 mile, the house at **4201 Tazewell**, on the left, with the long front porch, was built about 1928. The large brick house with slate roof 0.2 mile farther, at **4221 Tazewell**, is a 1928 Barber & McMurry house.

In 0.3 mile more, you'll see on the right the **Shannondale Presbyterian Church** at 4600 Tazewell Pike, built in 1886. Just before the church, you will have left the Knoxville City Limits. But continue a little farther into the county and you'll see several large homes dating from the late 1800s and early 1900s.

You'll see in 0.3 mile a log house at **4908 Tazewell** that dates from about 1850 and was probably a residence. The house next to it was built about 1910. Across from the log house, at 4909 Tazewell, you'll see the **Grassy Valley Homestead**.

In another 0.1 mile, at 5016 Tazewell Pike on the right, stands the **Truan House**, a frame house in the Four Square style built in 1883 and recommended for the National Register. The Truans were French-Swiss who had settled in the region. Just past the Truan House, where now you'll find a new subdivision, there once stood another home of a French-Swiss immigrant, Auguste Gouffon. The two-story log **Gouffon House**, built in 1849, was probably the oldest house in the area. The house was demolished. At 0.2 mile past the Truan House, you'll find on the left a **Victorian cottage** with elaborate detailing.

At a convenient place, turn around and return along Tazewell Pike 1.8 miles from the Truan House to Kesterwood Road on your right, which is across from the northeast end of Greenwood Cemetery. Turn on Kesterwood Road, then in 0.2 mile turn left on Kesterwood Drive; the neighborhood is made up of homes built in the early 1900s. In 0.2 mile turn right on Jacksboro Pike to Gibbs Drive in another 0.1 mile. Turn left on

Gibbs. The original homes along Gibbs Drive were constructed during the 1920s. In 0.6 mile from the beginning of Gibbs, just before you rejoin Broadway, a large yellow brick mansion stands on your right at 2805 Gibbs. This is the **Dempster Home**, the residence of George Dempster, the popular mayor of Knoxville 1952-55 and the inventor of the Dempster Dumpster for collecting trash. The mansion, with Ionic columns and a stone surrounding wall, was built about 1910.

At Broadway, turn north. In 0.2 mile, turn right at Essary Drive. You'll pass on your left **Litton's Market and Restaurant** where you'll find probably the best hamburger in town. In 0.6 mile when you get to Jacksboro Pike, turn left. You'll pass the new **Central High School** on your left in 0.2 mile. In another 0.2 mile, you'll see the entrance to **Harrill Hills** on the right, a subdivision with many homes constructed in the 1930s. To tour part of Harrill Hills, turn right on Grove Circle. Pass Terrace View and bear right on Dogwood to Briercliff Road. Turn left and then left again at Crestwood. Continue across Garden on Crestwood. Turn right on Forest Lane, and then bear right on Briercliff. When you reach Garden again, turn right.

In 0.2 mile, you'll cross Jacksboro Pike. As you continue on Garden, you'll see some homes that predate Harrill Hills. Several of the homes were built in 1905-10. In 0.3 mile on your right, notice the copper-top pagoda in **Savage Gardens** at 3227 Garden. The gardens were constructed about 1910 by Arthur Savage, considered the father of rock gardening in Knoxville.

As you descend toward Broadway on Garden, notice the large Bungalows on your left. Garden curves to the right to join Broadway in 0.2 mile from Savage Gardens. Turn left to return to Fountain City Park and Hotel Road.

Dempster Home

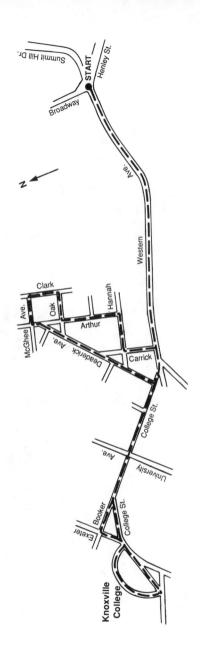

Mechanicsville and Knoxville College

11 Mechanicsville and Knoxville College Tour

3.3 miles
Connections: Market Square Walk, World's Fair Park

Attractions: You'll find in Mechanicsville a mix of large Victorian homes and worker cottages that make up one of Knoxville's earliest communities, which is near Knoxville College.

Start: Begin your driving tour of Mechanicsville at the intersection of Broadway, Western Avenue, Summit Hill Drive, and Henley Street on the Market Square Walk.

Description: Most of Knoxville's heavy industry in the mid-1800s was located northwest of the city center near the railroad tracks and the Second Creek area north of Western Avenue. The largest was the Knoxville Iron Company founded soon after the Civil War by Hiram S. Chamberlain, a Union Army captain from Ohio who was chief quartermaster at Knoxville during the war. Chamberlain provided the business sense, and several Welsh ironmasters came to the area to provide the technical expertise. Newly freed slaves provided much of the labor for the iron foundry.

A community grew up near the Knoxville Iron Company, the railroad shops, and other heavy industry in the area. In the late 1800s, an important railcar rebuilding facility, called "Coster Shops," was added to the area's industries. Coster Shops is still located north of the city center just east of I-275.

One of the first residential districts in this northwest area of the city was McGhee's Addition, a suburb developed by Charles McClung McGhee, a businessman whose large mansion still stands on Locust Street in the city center. The neighborhood grew with the addition of other suburbs, the Middleton and Weatherford Addition, Deaderick's Addition, Swann's Addition, and the Moses-Fairview Addition.

113

Part of the community became known as "Mechanicsville" because of the many "mechanics," or skilled artisans, that lived there and worked in the nearby factories. In these early years, the neighborhood was a mix of the Welsh ironmasters, factory owners, and businessmen with the workers and laborers in the industry—an economically and racially integrated community. The owners and businessmen built elaborate Queen Anne and Italianate residences while the workers lived in smaller cottages and houses. The community was served by a streetcar that ran through the neighborhood.

Although Mechanicsville was nearly a self-sufficient community with stores and other businesses and schools and churches, it never incorporated. Because of the lack of public services, the citizens of Mechanicsville petitioned the Knoxville Board of Mayor and Aldermen to accept the community as a part of Knoxville. Mechanicsville was annexed to the city in 1883. At the time the community had a population of around 2,000 people.

In later years, the industries declined and moved away, and soon the more well-to-do moved to the newer suburbs of Knoxville to the north and west. Mechanicsville subsequently suffered the same decline as other inner city neighborhoods; many houses were converted to rental units with the usual accompanying neglect.

Renewed interest in preservation of the neighborhood in recent years has contributed to a reversal of that deterioration. You'll see the results of many rehabilitation projects as you tour the community. This preservation effort led to the designation of Mechanicsville as an historic district on the National Register of Historic Places with 93 contributing structures.

To begin your tour, take Western Avenue west from the Henley, Broadway, Summit Hill intersection. You'll pass in front of the **L&N Railroad Station** in the World's Fair Park and over the **Western Avenue Viaduct**. Below the viaduct sits the building that was the **Knoxville Iron Company foundry**. In 0.6 mile, you'll reach College Street; bear left. Notice in the junction of College and Western the triangular commercial building at **1524 Western**, built about 1900.

In 0.1 mile after turning on College, turn right on Deaderick. At **209 Deaderick**, on the left, stands a two-story Queen Anne

114

house built about 1900; this was the home of W. J. Cansler, principal of Maynard School in the area. On the right at **220 Deaderick**, you'll find a restored two-story Victorian Vernacular home, and then at **224** you'll see another two-story residence, this one with Gothic Revival influence, also built about 1900.

On the left at **235 Deaderick** is another 1900 two-story Queen Anne home. On the right at **236-238** is another renovated Victorian. At **242**, notice the corner windows at the restored 1890 two-story home and the elaborate detailing using Hs, Os, Xs, and Is. Look for the low iron fence in front of the 1890 Queen Anne with Eastlake detailing at **243**. You'll see much ironwork in the neighborhood in railings and low fences; most of this was made at the Knoxville Iron Company. At **244**, you'll find a 1902 brick commercial building constructed in a wedge shape to fit in the triangle created by Deaderick and Carrick Streets.

On the right at the corner of Carrick and Deaderick stands the old **Moses School** at 220 Carrick Street, designed by R. F. Graf and Sons, built in 1916, and named for Col. John L. Moses, who in 1875 gave a tract of land to the community for the benefit of the neighborhood's black people; Fairview School was constructed on the land. The Moses School, now called the "Moses Center," houses the Knoxville Police Training Academy and acts as an incubation center for small businesses. This is also the headquarters for **Theatre Knoxville, Inc.**, which puts on plays in the Moses Center Auditorium. You'll find in the lobby of the Center the bell that once stood atop a school tower. The 2,000-pound bell was cast by the Meneely Bell Company of Troy, New York.

On the left, you'll pass **Trinity Chapel**, which is on the site of the Deaderick Avenue Baptist Church that was at one time the largest church in Knoxville. On the right, notice the iron railings below and above the front window of an old two-story house. Again on the left, just past Trinity Chapel, you'll see an old Vernacular home with Italianate influences, and then at **401 Deaderick**, you'll find a Victorian cottage probably designed by George Barber.

At Arthur Street, bear left to the corner with McGhee Avenue. On the southwest corner stands **Fire Station No. 5**, the oldest remaining fire station in Knoxville and now on the

National Register. It was built in 1909 in the Italian Villa style. Notice the short tower at the top of the building, which was used for hanging cloth fire hoses for drying. The old pumper fire truck that operated out of the station is now on display in front of the Fire Department Headquarters on Summit Hill Drive in the city center.

Turn right on McGhee. At **1012** and **1008 McGhee** on the right are shotgun houses built about 1900. These worker houses with rooms aligned front to back are called "shotgun" because when you stand on the front porch and look through the house with all the doors open, it's like looking down the barrel of a shotgun.

When you reach Clark Street at the next corner, turn right. At **417 Clark Street**, on the right, you'll see another cottage, and then at **415 Clark** is an elaborate one-story frame house with a sunburst design in the porch gable. When you reach Oak Street, turn right.

At **1007 Oak Street**, on the right, stands a finely restored two-story Queen Anne with Eastlake detailing on the porch, built around 1890. Architect Gene Burr aided in the renovation of this house. At **1013 Oak**, you'll see a two-story house with large Ionic columns that was the home of Alvin Webber, the owner of a Mechanicsville furniture store.

At Arthur Street, turn left. In 0.2 mile, turn right on Hannah, where you'll see several workers' cottages. At Carrick Street, turn left. On your left at the corner of Carrick and Hannah, notice the one and a half-story Queen Anne cottage at **122 Carrick**, built about 1890. And then at the end of the block, stand two turn-of-the-century townhouses on the left that are mirror images of each other.

At the end of Carrick at Western Avenue, turn right to head toward Knoxville College. Bear right again on College Street, and in 0.2 mile, you'll cross University Avenue. You'll pass **Maynard Elementary School** on the right. Then as you approach the college, notice the triangle formed by College, Exeter, and Booker Streets which contains several brick houses that served as faculty housing for the college. Bear left at the triangle, and at 0.2 mile from University Avenue, turn right into the Knoxville College Campus.

1007 Oak Street

Knoxville College was founded in 1875 by the United Presbyterian Church as a school for blacks in Knoxville. It moved to this location in 1876. It remained a black college until in 1954 the charter was amended to permit white students to attend. Today, the college remains a predominantly black institution that has continued to serve the black population of the city and the state. It was through sit-in demonstrations in the city center in the 1960s that Knoxville College students and faculty brought about integration of public facilities in Knoxville. In 1979, the United Presbyterian Church deeded the college property to the Board of Trustees of Knoxville College.

As you proceed around the college drive, you'll see on the right **McMillan Chapel**, built in 1913, the **Alumni Library**, constructed in 1966, and then **Elnathan Hall**, built in 1893 for offices and classrooms. Bear to the left to continue around the curved drive and see **McKee Hall**, an administration building constructed in 1895, and **Wallace Hall**, built in 1890.

When you reach College Street again, notice to the right the one and a half-story Bungalow, built about 1906, at **1005 College**, that serves as a faculty residence. Turn left on College Street, and just past the entrance to the college, bear left on Exeter Avenue. You'll see just on your left the **College President's Residence** at 1605 Exeter, built in 1886-89 of wood but rebuilt with brick in 1905.

At the next corner, turn right on Booker Street, which rejoins College at the next corner. Continue straight on College 1.5 miles back to Western and back to the city center.

McKee Hall (David Cann)

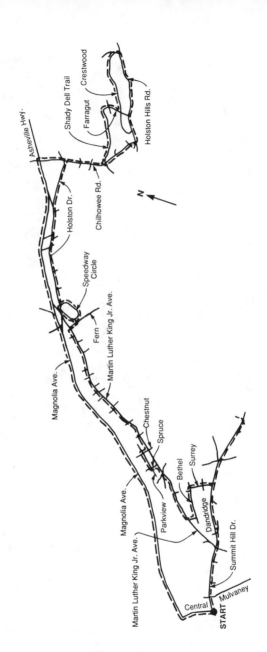

East Knoxville and Holston Hills

12 East Knoxville and Holston Hills Tour

16 miles
Connections: Chilhowee Park, Park City Tour

Attractions: This tour takes you by historic homes in the once incorporated community of East Knoxville and the Holston Hills subdivision.

Start: Begin on Summit Hill Drive headed east from Central Street.

Description: The City of Knoxville initially grew from the original sixteen blocks to cover the hill confined between First Creek on the east and Second Creek on the west plus the Tennessee River on the south. The northern boundary was gradually extended to include Old Gray Cemetery, which is north of the city center on Broadway.

Several communities grew up adjacent to this small City of Knoxville. The first of these communities to reach the status of a separate town was East Knoxville that had grown up on the east side of First Creek.

As the community of East Knoxville took shape, access to the east was necessary. The first bridge across First Creek to connect the growing community with the city was constructed in 1819. East Knoxville was incorporated in 1856. Other bridges were built between the two cities as the two municipalities increased their cooperation. Finally, East Knoxville was annexed by the City of Knoxville in 1868.

Blacks have long been a part of East Knoxville, as they have been in other neighborhoods in the city. In 1869, David Brown was elected city alderman from the East Knoxville community, the first black alderman for Knoxville. Over the years, black residents of the city tended to move into East Knoxville, creating some neighborhoods and a community of small businesses that are predominantly black. With time, because of the lack of economic opportunity for residents in East Knoxville, some neighborhoods deteriorated so that in the 1950s and 1960s the Knoxville Housing Authority instituted urban renewal projects that cleared several neighborhoods east of the city center and channelized First Creek to prevent the flooding that had frequently occurred.

You'll encounter one of these projects as you begin your tour of East Knoxville by taking Summit Hill Drive east of the city center. After crossing over the Business Loop, you'll be in the Mountain View urban renewal project area. The 184 acres of the project now has the city's auditorium/coliseum, the safety building, parking garages, a school, public housing, and parks. You'll see none of the old residences, churches, and business buildings, because the first urban renewal projects swept everything away. Later projects used partial clearance combined with rehabilitation of buildings worth saving.

Cal Johnson Park is to the right on Mulvaney Street. The park was established about 1922 and named for Caldonia F. Johnson, a prominent black businessman in the late 1800s who was proprietor of a saloon called "The Poplar Log." Located at the corner of Gay Street and Vine Avenue, the establishment was frequented by the city's leading men. Johnson was born a slave of one of the McClung families. After being freed with the coming of the Civil War, he rose to a position in which he owned much real estate, including the city's only horse race track, and several thoroughbred horses. In 1883, he was a member of the city's Board of Aldermen. With the construction of the Downtown Loop and the **Knoxville Chamber of Commerce** at the corner of Mulvaney and Church Street, Cal Johnson Park was reduced in size. But you'll still find here tennis courts and the Cal Johnson Recreation Center.

Continue past Mulvaney on Summit Hill Drive as it becomes Dandridge Avenue at 0.6 mile from the start of the tour. You'll see **Morningside Park** on your right. On your left at 1711 Dandridge, 0.2 mile from the beginning of Dandridge, stands the **Mabry-Hazen House**, a two-story Italianate with Greek Revival influence built in 1858. Because of its history and its unique architecture, the house has been listed on the National Register of

Mabry-Hazen House

Historic Places. The house was originally the residence of Joseph Mabry, who with William Swan gave the area of Market Square to the city in 1853. During the Civil War, the house was occupied by both Confederate and Union troops. In the early 1900s, it was the home of Rush Strong Hazen and his wife, Alice Evelyn Mabry, the daughter of Joseph Mabry. Hazen was for years in the wholesale grocery business and was later president and chairman of the board of the Morris Plan Bank that became the Tennessee Valley Bank. The Hazens' daughter, Evelyn Hazen, provided for restoration of the house after her death. The Mabry-Hazen House is being restored by the Hazen Historical Museum Foundation, Inc., with Frank Sparkman as architect, and should be open to the public in the spring of 1991.

At 1927 Dandridge, on the left, in another 0.3 mile, you'll find the **Beck Cultural Exchange Center**, a museum of black history and culture that serves as one of the state repositories for black history. Open to the public, the Beck Center has an art gallery, a library/research center, and the William Henry Hastie Room that contains a permanent collection of memorabilia of the Knoxville native that became the first black federal judge and the first black governor of the Virgin Islands. The center is named for James and Ethel Beck, prominent members of the community who once lived in the 1912 house the center occupies and who, on their death, left a sum of money that the community used to establish the center.

Continue on Dandridge 0.3 mile to the crossing of Wilder Place and with Brooks Road to the left and Dandridge to the right. Keep on Dandridge 0.4 mile to 2325 Dandridge where you'll find the **Col. John Williams House**, built around 1815 and now on the National Register. Williams served with Andrew Jackson during the 1814 Creek War, during which time they became political rivals. Williams was a U. S. Senator in 1815, but was defeated for reelection by Jackson in 1823. In later years the house was purchased by the state for a branch of the Tennessee School for the Deaf for black children. The state-owned house is now on the grounds of the Sertoma Learning Center, a private nonprofit agency that provides work training for the handicapped. The house is sealed to help preserve it until funds and an appropriate use can be found for its restoration. On the Sertoma grounds, you
124

can visit the center's greenhouse and ceramics shop.

From the Williams house turn around and return along Dandridge 0.7 mile to Surrey Street. Turn right to Bethel Avenue. You'll find the **Odd Fellows Cemetery** across Bethel. Odd Fellows was a fraternal order. The cemetery contains many of Knoxville's black leaders.

Turn left on Bethel Avenue, and you'll see on the right the **Confederate Cemetery** where more than 1600 Confederate soldiers were buried. The cemetery was established in 1873 so that the remains of Confederates buried hastily around the city during the war could be reburied in an honored place. W. D. Winstead, a Confederate soldier, became superintendent of the cemetery. He and his family lived in the small 1886 house you can see inside the gate. The cemetery was eventually deeded to the Winstead family. The daughter, Mamie Winstead, on her death in 1989 left the house and cemetery to the Hazen Historical Museum Foundation, which may soon open the house and cemetery to the public. You'll notice on the grounds a 48-foot high monument topped by a Confederate soldier facing north, designed by the noted local artist Lloyd Branson.

On the other side of the Confederate Cemetery is **Calvary Catholic Cemetery**. This area that includes the three cemeteries also at one time included a "Potter's Field," established in the 1800s by the city for its indigent.

At the end of the block, turn right on Bertrand to Martin Luther King Jr. Avenue. Across the avenue stands **Vine Middle School**, and far to your left, you can see the old **Austin High School**. Built in 1928, the high school was named for Emily Austin, who came from Philadelphia in 1870 to educate blacks in Knoxville; by 1885 she had established the Slater Training School. Vine Junior High School was established in the high school building when a new Austin High School was constructed nearby in 1952, the building now occupied by Vine Middle School. Austin High operated there until the late 1960s when school desegregation programs merged Austin High with the white East High School, and Vine Junior moved from the original high school to this newer school and became Vine Middle.

Turn right on King Avenue. After traveling by the three cemeteries, you'll pass **Walter Hardy City Park** on the right, named for a black physician who worked in the neighborhood, and the **Tabernacle Baptist Church** on the left and in half a mile reach Five Points, where five streets come together. Just past the intersection, turn left on Spruce Street. At Parkview Avenue turn right. At the end of the next block, notice at 2460 Parkview the **Bethel African Methodist Episcopal Church**; the church was established around 1900 and moved to this location in the mid-1900s. Turn right on Chestnut Street to return to Martin Luther King Jr. Avenue, and then turn left.

At 2639 King, on your left in 0.2 mile, notice **Mount Rest Home**, founded by the Women's Educational and Industrial Union as a home for destitute elderly women. The house Mount Rest occupies was built for Joseph Mabry, Jr., who named it "Mount Rest." The house later was the residence of the first sheriff of Knox County, Robert Houston, who called his place "Cold Spring Farm." The house was enlarged and reassumed its original name when it was converted to Mount Rest Home.

Continue out King Avenue for 0.4 mile, and at 2800 King you'll find on your right **Austin-East High School**, which is the combination of Austin and East High Schools.

As you continue east on King Street, you will enter the community of Burlington. You'll pass on the left the **Burlington Branch Library** of the Knox County Public Library System. On your right at 0.7 mile past Austin-East, stands the **Warner Tabernacle AME Zion Church**, established in 1848 and now occupying what had been the McCalla Avenue Baptist Church, with an older sanctuary on the right.

Just after the church turn right on Fern Street and then left on Calvin to **Speedway Circle**, a half-mile circular drive that traces the old horse race track of Cal Johnson. The Speedway now is lined with homes constructed in the 1920s and 1930s.

After circling the Speedway, get off on Holston Drive, which skirts Speedway Circle on the north and continue heading east. At one mile bear right, and you'll enter **Chilhowee Hills** subdivision and reach Chilhowee Road in another 0.3 mile.

Turn right, and in 0.2 mile you'll enter **Holston Hills**, a subdivision along the Holston River above the confluence of the Holston and the French Broad that was annexed to the city in 1962. At the end of Chilhowee Road, a half mile from the

Mount Rest

entrance to Holston Hills, turn left on Holston Hills Road that passes along the northern side of **Holston Hills Country Club**, constructed in 1926 from a Barber & McMurry design resembling English Tudor. The houses along Holston Hills Road on your left were built in the 1920s and several have been recommended for the National Register. Pass Crestwood Drive and Farragut Drive until at 0.7 mile from the country club you'll reach an intersection with the other end of Crestwood to the left. Turn up Crestwood to Farragut in 0.6 mile. Turn right on Farragut. When you cross Green Valley Road, Farragut becomes Shady Dell Trail, which at its end in half a mile joins Chilhowee Road. Turn right to leave Holston Hills.

Keep on Chilhowee until you reach Asheville Highway in 0.6 mile; across the highway you'll see **Chilhowee Elementary School**. Turn left on Asheville Highway to head back toward the city center. As you pass back through Burlington, Asheville Highway curves left and becomes Magnolia Avenue. On your right, at 2.1 miles from Chilhowee Road, you'll come to **Chilhowee Park**, where fairs and other gatherings are held, and the **Knoxville Zoological Park**, which is behind Chilhowee on Prosser Road. If you want to enter Chilhowee Park, turn right on Beaman Street to get to the entrance. At Beaman you are also at the end of the Park City Tour.

From Chilhowee Park, continue west on Magnolia. At 0.7 mile from the park, notice on the left the **Magnolia Avenue United Methodist Church**, a Gothic Revival built about 1926. In another 1.4 miles, you'll see **Bill Meyer Stadium** to the right on Jessamine Street, where the Knoxville Bluejays play baseball.

In another half mile, just before reaching Central Street, notice at the corner of Magnolia and Morgan the **Peabody School** at 311 Morgan Street on the left, a red-brick building that was the first building constructed as a public school in Knoxville, built in 1874. It was named to recognize the early support of schools by the Peabody Fund. The building now houses the Painters Local Union of the AFL/CIO.

At the intersection of Magnolia with Central Street, you can turn left to pass through Old City to your starting point on Summit Hill Drive. You can also turn right to the beginning of the Park City Tour.

5405 Holston Hills Road

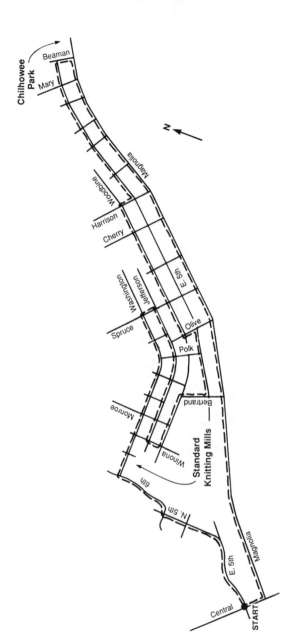

Park City

130

⅓ Park City Tour

8 miles
Connections: East Knoxville Tour, Chilhowee Park, Emory
Place and the 4th and Gill Neighborhood Walk

Attractions: The Park City community consists of the neighborhoods that once constituted the incorporated town of Park City. You'll find here many turn-of-the-century homes, including probably the largest collection of George Barber homes in the country.

Start: Start at the corner of Central Street and 5th Avenue north of the city center and just south of Emory Place. From here, you can also connect with the Emory Place/4th and Gill Neighborhood Walk. Drive east on 5th Avenue.

Description: In addition to the suburban neighborhoods that grew up north of Knoxville's city center during the early years of economic expansion, neighborhoods took shape east of the city as well. Residential development in the Park City area that lay north of East Knoxville began about the time streetcar lines were extended into the neighborhood in the early 1890s. Only scattered residential development had occurred before this time. The streetcar lines ran along what was then Park Avenue, later named "Magnolia," and along Washington Avenue. In 1892 the Edgewood Land and Improvement Company subdivided land along Washington Avenue and began selling lots in the first planned development. Residential construction continued until about 1940.

The neighborhood was laid out as a typical streetcar suburb—long blocks with streets running parallel to the streetcar line. The first residents were merchants and professionals who occupied large, elaborate homes. Smaller homes were constructed in later developments, where resided clerks, salesman, and workers in Knoxville's factories, mills, and railroads. The plants of Standard Knitting Mills, one of the largest employers in the area, formed the western boundary of the neighborhood. The eastern boundary was Chilhowee Park, from which Park City got its name.

Early on, the City of Knoxville attempted to annex part of the area when it created the Tenth Ward in 1891. But only two years later, the Tenth Ward was removed from the boundaries of the city because of opposition to annexation among the people living in the neighborhoods and because the city had failed to provide adequate services. In 1907, the community incorporated into its own municipality, calling itself "Park City." But the City of Knoxville could not long ignore the fast growing community and annexed the entire neighborhood in 1917.

Park City, or "Parkridge" as it came to be known during the urban renewal era, suffered the same economic pressures during the 1930s as the neighborhoods to the north. Then in the 1950s, the textile industry experienced a decline, and there were large cuts in employment. The young middle class began relocating to newer subdivisions, and the neighborhood began to deteriorate. In the 1960s, urban renewal projects near the city center caused a dislocation of people eastward into Park City, with resulting population changes, and the construction of I-40 through the city center created a barrier between Park City and neighborhoods to the north, which tended to isolate Park City from much of the Knoxville community.

In recent years, with the increased emphasis on neighborhood improvement and the tendency for young middle class with historic preservation in mind to relocate in architecturally significant homes in old neighborhoods, the decline of Park City is beginning to be reversed. Neighborhood organizations are working to improve the community, and homes are being restored. Park City has recently been nominated to the National Register of Historic Places as the Park City Historic District, which contains 891 contributing structures including elaborate Queen Anne homes on the west to Bungalow and Craftsman residences on the east.

Begin your tour headed east on 5th Avenue from the corner of Central Street. In 0.3 mile you'll cross Randolph; bear left on N. 5th Avenue 0.3 mile to the corner of 6th Avenue. Notice the house at **725 N. 5th Avenue**, built about 1880, and the house at

132

777, built about 1904. Turn right on 6th 0.3 mile to Washington Avenue. Along the way, you'll pass the **6th Avenue Baptist Church**. At the corner of Washington and 6th there once stood an **Electric Generating Plant**, built in 1900. This was the first coal-fired electric generating plant in Knoxville. The building was eligible for the National Register. It was demolished in July 1990. Turn right on Washington, again headed east.

Along Washington Avenue, you'll see **Standard Knitting Mills** on your right. The old multistory brick mill buildings, constructed about 1900 in the Victorian Vernacular style, are eligible for listing on the National Register.

As you proceed down Washington Avenue across Mitchell and Winona Streets, you'll enter the section of Park City developed by the Edgewood Land and Improvement Company. One of the developers involved with the Edgewood company was Martin E. Parmelee, at one time the partner of George Barber in the architectural firm of Barber and Parmelee. In 0.1 mile past Winona, on your left, you'll reach the first of several Barber houses at **1635 Washington Avenue**.

George F. Barber set up offices in Knoxville in the 1880s after moving to the city from Illinois. He advertised his house designs in catalogs he sold all over the U. S. Barber and his firms produced over 20,000 sets of house plans. A person could not only order house plans, but the house itself. Presumably Barber located in Knoxville because the city provided the rail transportation he needed to ship his prefabricated houses.

In 1888, Barber formed a partnership with Martin Parmelee and became involved in designing many of the homes in Park City. Barber's partnerships changed over time, but one of the most prominent was Barber and Kluttz. Barber's son, Charles, eventually joined the firm and also became a famous architect, designing many homes and commercial and public buildings as part of the firm of Barber & McMurry.

The George Barber homes in Park City range from Queen Anne and Eastlake styles to Colonial Revival and Neoclassical designs with some Richardsonian Romanesque influences. There are sixteen Barber houses in the neighborhood, perhaps more since the location of all Barber houses in Knoxville is not known. This constitutes perhaps the largest concentration of Barber

133

1635 Washington Avenue

houses anywhere in the country.

Barber lived in the house he designed at 1635 Washington Avenue. Although the house retains much of its elaborate detail, missing are the roof crest, corner turret, and chimneys. The house at **1702** is also a Barber house. The homes at **1704** and **1712** are likely his also. He also lived for a time in the house at **1724 Washington**. Other Barber houses are at **1730**, **1802**, and **1803 Washington Avenue**. The house at **1806** is a likely Barber house; **1912 Washington Avenue** is a Barber.

At the southeast corner of Washington Avenue and Polk Street, you'll see **Refuge Temple**, which was originally a Quaker church, built about 1925. The Queen Anne house at **2041 Washington** was designed and built in 1893 by John Ryno, who worked in the Barber firm and later became a well-known architect in the firm Ryno & Brackney.

Continue on Washington to Spruce Street. Turn right and at the next corner turn right on Jefferson Avenue. Notice the nicely restored Victorian house with Shingle influence on the left at **2320 Jefferson** and the Queen Anne also on the left at **2038**, after crossing Polk Avenue. On the right at **1731 Jefferson** is a house that is probably a Barber design. A Barber Queen Anne with Eastlake detailing stands at **1701 Jefferson**. The residence at **1640**, on the left after you cross Monroe, is probably a Barber house. Notice the restored house at **1619 Jefferson**, on the right. Then at **1603** is another likely Barber house. Turn left on Winona, and at the next corner turn left on Woodbine Avenue.

In 0.2 mile turn right on Bertrand Street. On your right at 523 Bertrand, you'll find **Park Place**, a condominium complex in what was the old Park Junior High School, built in 1926-27. The school was designed by Baumann and Baumann with consulting architect William B. Itner, a school specialist located in St. Louis. The renovation to Park Place was another project of Kristopher and Company. The building is on the National Register.

At the next corner, turn left on E. 5th Avenue. On your right stands the **Greater Ebenezer Baptist Church**, at 1912 E. 5th Avenue, built about 1922 with Gothic detailing; notice the cast iron lamp posts that mark the entrance. You'll see an American Four Square at **1929 E. 5th Avenue**, on the left, and also at **2003** and **2007**. At Olive Street, turn left, and at the next corner turn

Park Place

136

right on Woodbine. Notice the Tudor Revival at **2305 Woodbine**. Many houses of Minimal Traditional style, in which minimal detailing is used, are along this 2300 block of Woodbine. The house at **2336** was the first Florence Crittenton Home in Knoxville, established in 1896. Providing a refuge for young women and girls, the agency still operates in Knoxville. The house on Woodbine was sold to the agency for a dollar by Maj. E. C. Camp, who built Greystone on Broadway. The Woodbine house is now a private residence. After crossing Spruce, you'll see another likely Barber house at **2458 Woodbine**.

Cross Chestnut and Cherry Streets. At the next corner turn right on Harrison Street one block to E. 5th Avenue. The house at the corner, on your left, **2701 E. 5th Avenue**, is a house in which Barber used both Neoclassical and Colonial Revival design elements that were typical of his later designs. Turn left on 5th. In this later section of Park City, you'll see many Bungalow and Craftsman style homes. But also notice the Spanish Eclectic on the right at **2806 E. 5th**, the Colonial Revival at **2900 E. 5th**, and the Dutch Colonial Revival on the left at **2915 E. 5th**.

At **3105 E. Fifth**, on the right, you'll see a Craftsman style house with Prairie influences. Watch on the left for the Bungalow with oriental influence and the angled walk to the corner at **3201** at the corner with Mary Street.

At the end of 5th Avenue at Beaman Street, you will be across from the entrance to Chilhowee Park. Turn right on Beaman to Magnolia Avenue. At this junction, you will have joined the end of the East Knoxville Tour. Turn right on Magnolia to return to the city center at Central Street.

Magnolia Avenue was once a part of the residential district of Park City, but commercial development has since changed the makeup of the structures along the avenue. Still, you'll see old apartment buildings and residences among the commercial structures. The avenue was named for Magnolia Bryan Branner, the mother of H. Bryan Branner, the mayor of Knoxville in 1880. The Branner family home stood on the site of the present **Knoxville Catholic High School** at 1610 Magnolia at 1.8 miles from Beaman Street.

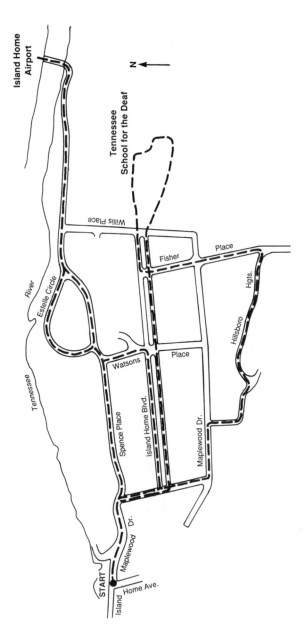

Island Home Park

138

14 Island Home Park Walk

3.5 miles
Connections: Ijams Park

Attractions: This walk through the Island Home Park community takes you by Bungalow style homes built in the early 1900s and the Tennessee School for the Deaf that contains the old Dickinson country place, "Island Home."

Start: From the south end of Gay Street in the city center, cross the Gay Street Bridge over the Tennessee River and turn left on Sevier Avenue. Along the way, notice the Gothic structure on the other side of the river that is one of the first water plants for Knoxville, built in the 1920s. At 0.7 mile, when Sevier bears to the right, continue straight on Island Home Avenue. In 0.7 mile from Sevier Avenue, Island Home turns to the right. Straight ahead is Island Home Park on Maplewood, the starting place for this walk. If you were to continue on Island Home Avenue, you would reach Ijams Park in 1.3 miles.

Description: The communities that took shape in South Knoxville were at first isolated by the Tennessee River that separated the settlements from the city center. Ferry service provided some means for the people of South Knoxville to get to the business center of the city. But the area remained for a time so isolated it was referred to as "South America."

After the Union occupation during the Civil War, the county acquired the pontoon bridge the Union Army had constructed across the river, but it was washed away by a flood in 1867. A new bridge was built, but it was blown away by fierce winds in 1875. A third bridge was built in 1880, and then the present bridge was constructed in 1897-98, finally providing a permanent link to the South Knoxville neighborhoods.

The communities south of the river were annexed to the city in 1917. The Henley Street Bridge, constructed in 1930 as part of a scenic highway to the Great Smoky Mountains to the southeast,

139

provided more access. Even so, South Knoxville remains a place apart, quiet neighborhoods within a few miles drive of the city center.

One of these neighborhoods, **Island Home Park**, was the creation of the Island Home Park Company, which in the early 1900s developed the neighborhood as a subdivision for Knoxville. Begin your walk at the stone pillars marking the entrance to Island Home Park on Maplewood Drive.

The first house on the right at **1900 Maplewood** was already in existence at the time of the park development; it was built around 1880 but has since been altered. The next two homes at **1932** and **1936 Maplewood**, built in 1913 and 1915, are two of the earliest homes. The remaining homes in the park were built from 1915 to about 1930.

Soon after entering the park, Maplewood Drive curves to the right while Spence Place leads straight ahead. Stay with Maplewood and you'll soon come to Island Home Boulevard, a half-mile drive with a median of grass and dogwood trees that bloom white and pink in the spring. At one time a streetcar ran down the median of Island Home Boulevard.

As you walk the length of Island Home Boulevard, watch for the residence on the right at 2144 that is the **Cullum House**, the childhood home of John Cullum, a nationally known actor who got his start at the University of Tennessee's Carousel Theater. Also watch for the home on the left at **2237** that was the first house on the Boulevard, built about 1915.

At the end of the boulevard, you'll find the entrance to the **Tennessee School for the Deaf** at 2725 Island Home Boulevard. The School for the Deaf was established by the Tennessee legislature in 1844; at the time it was unfortunately called the "Tennessee Deaf and Dumb School" and was often referred to as the "Deaf and Dumb Asylum." The school first met in an East Knoxville residence, but in 1851 a large school building was completed on land west of the city center given to the school by Calvin Morgan, a successful merchant. After the school moved to Island Home in 1924, the old buildings on the campus became Knoxville's City Hall; today that complex on Summit Hill Drive serves as offices for the Tennessee Valley Authority. A year after the move to Island Home, the name of the school was changed.

140

The 125 acres that make up the school campus are part of what was once **Island Home**, the country home of Perez Dickinson. The brother-in-law of East Tennessee College President Joseph Estabrook, Dickinson came to Knoxville in 1829 to be principal at Hampden-Sidney Academy and attend East Tennessee College. He soon gave up his teaching career and joined with another brother-in-law, James Cowan, in a mercantile firm that later was organized into Cowan, McClung and Company, probably the largest wholesale business in the region. Dickinson worked as part of that firm as well as owning his own wholesale company. He prospered and became president of the First National Bank, the first president of the Knoxville Board of Trade, and a trustee of East Tennessee University. He lived in a great mansion on Main Avenue in the city center. But he also wanted a country house, and in 1869 he purchased Williams Island and with other land established a 600-acre model farm that became known as "Island Home." Island Home Boulevard was once the entrance to the farm. The mansion that was Dickinson's country home served as the residence for the superintendent of the Tennessee School for the Deaf from 1924 to 1986; it is now the residence of the Director of Student Living. Williams Island became known as Dickinson Island, where Island Home Airport is now located.

To see the Island Home mansion, check in at the guard gate at the school and walk up the hill on the school's grounds. You'll see the large white mansion on your left. Dickinson either had the home constructed or had an existing home remodeled in the early 1870s. You'll be able to walk around the mansion by turning left just past the home and following the drive to return to the school entrance.

As you make the turn along the back of the house, you'll see on your right the **Hershel Ward Building**, built in 1924 and designed by Thomas Marr, a graduate of the Tennessee School for the Deaf who became an architect. There have been proposals to demolish the building.

After returning to the school entrance, walk one short block back along Island Home Boulevard and turn left on Fisher Place to see more of the homes of Island Home Park. Toward the end of Fisher at Island Home Avenue, you'll see on your left the

141

Dickinson Home

Island Home Baptist Church; you can walk around to the front or you'll get a better view of the building on a later drive to Ijams Park. The congregation was founded in 1860 as the Holston Baptist Church. In 1882, Perez Dickinson donated land for a church structure, and the name was changed with the construction of a new church building. The present building, on the same spot as the 1882 church, was constructed in 1922.

From the end of Fisher Place, return along Fisher one block to Hillsboro Heights and turn left, headed west. Bear right to stay on Hillsboro and then turn left on Maplewood Drive and return along Maplewood past Island Home Boulevard to Spence Place. Turn right on Spence, which is presumably named for Cary F. Spence who was a captain in the Spanish-American War, served with distinction as a colonel in World War I, and who was president of the Island Home Park Company in the early years.

You can walk all the way to **Island Home Airport** at the end of Spence Place on Dickinson Island in 0.7 mile; you'll cross a bridge over a side channel of the Tennessee River to get to the island. The airport is a city airport for private planes. From the island, return along Spence Place to reenter the Island Home Park neighborhood.

To complete the walk, turn off Spence Place on the east end of Estelle Circle. You'll pass along the river on your right and then **Island Home Community Park**. When Estelle reconnects with Spence Place, turn right on Spence and then left on Watsons Place. You'll emerge in one block back on Island Home Boulevard. Turn right to return to Maplewood and then right again to walk back to the entrance to Island Home Park.

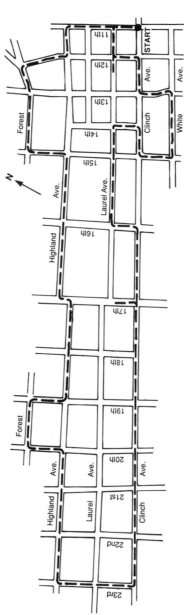

Fort Sanders

144

15 Fort Sanders Walk

3.0 miles
Connections: World's Fair Park Walk, The University of
Tennessee Campus Walk

Attractions: This tour takes you through the Fort Sanders neighborhood that at one time was the City of West Knoxville.

Start: Begin this walk from the Arts Center complex of the Candy Factory and the 11th Street Victorian houses, which is on the World's Fair Park Walk. To the south, at the corner of 11th Street and Cumberland Avenue, you can also connect with the University of Tennessee Campus Walk.

Description: During the Union occupation of Knoxville during the Civil War, most of the hills around the city were fortified, including The Hill where East Tennessee University was located, later the University of Tennessee, and a hill northwest of the university. The fortification on this other hill was named "Fort Loudoun."

In 1863, Confederate Lieutenant-General James Longstreet moved on Knoxville from the southwest, intending to retake the city. Union General William P. Sanders and his cavalry held off the Confederates along Kingston Pike while the fortification of Knoxville was completed. Then the siege of Knoxville began on November 17th with the Union troops retreating into the city.

Longstreet made his headquarters for the siege at Robert Armstrong's Kingston Pike residence, called "Bleak House." Sharpshooters were stationed in the tower of Bleak House, and on November 18th during a small skirmish, one of them was able to shoot General Sanders. Sanders was removed to a makeshift hospital in the Lamar House on Gay Street, but he died the next day. In his memory, Fort Loudoun was renamed "Fort Sanders."

Rather than waiting to starve the Union troops out of Knoxville, Longstreet decided to attack on November 29. The main assault was on Fort Sanders, which had been well fortified with earthworks, trenches, telegraph wire, and downed trees. The fort was manned by 220 Union soldiers, but after only 20 minutes of fighting, the Confederates retreated with 813 casualties while the fort's defenders lost only 13 men. The Union forces won other skirmishes around the city and effectively held Knoxville. Long-street withdrew, and the Union troops continued to hold Knoxville until the end of the war.

The south slope of the hill that was now Fort Sanders was the property of Hugh Andrew May White. In the 1870s White's heirs subdivided the property for a residential neighborhood, which became known as White's Addition. The area became an exclusive suburb, and many large homes were built in the latter part of the 19th century for industrialists and university staff. Ramsey's Addition was added to the north on the other side of Fort Sanders hill; this addition became a middle and lower-middle class neighborhood for craftsmen, small businessmen, and workers in the manufacturing and railroad industries.

The neighborhood was incorporated as the town of West Knoxville in 1888 but was annexed by Knoxville in 1897. With the 1930s Depression, many homeowners found it necessary to rent all or parts of their homes, unable to maintain the houses on their dwindling income. The trend to rental units increased as the University of Tennessee continued to grow and students sought housing off campus. The area began to decline as a neighborhood, and some of the old homes were razed to make way for apartment buildings.

Today, while the neighborhood remains a major residential area for university students and staff, there is a growing recognition of the value of the historic homes that remain. You'll see many efforts to renovate and preserve the remaining structures as you walk the neighborhood. This recognition and effort resulted in the neighborhood being designated an historic district on the National Register of Historic Places. The Fort Sanders Historic District contains over 300 contributing structures.

To begin your walk, head north on 11th Street from the Arts Center. Turn west on Highland Avenue into Ramsey's Addition. In this first block you'll see several Victorian Vernacular houses built in the late 1800s. Turn right on 12th Street; notice several

Vernacular homes on the right that have been restored for rental property. You'll find that 12th Street and, later, 13th Street are concrete, a street paving that was also used in the Old North Knoxville Neighborhood.

At Forest Avenue, turn left headed west. Cross 13th Street. At **1312** and **1316 Forest** on the left stand two Victorian Vernacular homes, built about 1905. On the right at **1401** is a Shingle cottage. At **1411 Forest** stands a Gothic cottage built in the 1880s.

At the corner of 15th Street, you'll see a low stone wall on the southeast corner; such walls are frequent in the Fort Sanders Neighborhood.

Turn left on 15th to Highland Avenue. The house on the northeast corner of 15th and Highland at **1415 Highland** was built about 1888 by J. J. Craig, Jr., who had joined his father in the John J. Craig and Company marble business. Notice the marble circles in the sidewalk in front of the house, which faces Highland.

Turn right on Highland, headed west. At **1509 Highland**, on the right, you'll find the Fountain Place Condominiums that stand on the site of the family home of James Agee, the noted author and critic who spent his early childhood in the Fort Sanders Neighborhood. Agee's novel, *A Death in the Family*, based on his father's death in a 1916 car accident, won the Pulitzer Prize in 1958.

The restored 1886 house at **1513 Highland** that is used as offices for the condominium complex has Shingle influences, a Victorian style characterized by covering the walls and roofs with shingles.

On the left at **1516 Highland** stands an 1886 Victorian Vernacular. The **East Tennessee Community Design Center** occupies the 1886 house at 1522 Highland. The Community Design Center is a consulting firm of volunteers who aid communities with few resources in developing parks, renovating historic sites, and providing affordable housing. The center grew out of the effort to preserve the Fort Sanders Neighborhood. Next to the center, stands a nicely restored two-story Queen Anne house, and you'll see a well-restored Queen Anne cottage at **1530**. At the

1513 Highland Avenue (David Cann)

148

corner stands **Christ Chapel** at 1538 Highland, built originally in 1907 and rebuilt in 1929 as the Epworth Methodist Episcopal Church South.

In the next block after crossing 16th Street, notice the houses on the right, all built in 1890-91 as residences for middle class homeowners. At **1645 Highland** notice the round Queen Anne porch. Turn left on 17th and then right to continue west on Highland Avenue. Cross 18th Street. At **1810 Highland**, notice the double porch and double bay window of this 1895 house.

At 19th Street turn right to Forest Avenue and then left on Forest. In this block, you'll see the smaller homes characteristic of the workers' homes nearer the base of the hill. Turn left on 20th Street to return to Highland and turn right.

Continue west on Highland to 23rd Street. You'll find in this west section of Fort Sanders a later development that includes many Bungalow style houses built in the 1920s and 1930s. Turn left on 23rd and top the hill at Laurel Avenue. Continue on 23rd down the hill to Clinch Avenue. When you reach Clinch, turn left. On the right at 21st Street, you'll find the **East Tennessee Children's Hospital** at 2018 Clinch Avenue. In the block between 20th and 19th streets, on the left, you'll pass in front of the **Fort Sanders Regional Medical Center**. The newer buildings replaced the original buildings of Fort Sanders Hospital that had been built in the early 1920s on part of the site of the old Civil War earthen fortification that was Fort Sanders. On the right, you'll also see the **Thompson Cancer Survival Center**

East on Clinch Avenue, you'll cross 19th Street and enter White's Addition where you'll see the more elaborate homes of Fort Sanders. Notice the brick Tudor Revival on the right at **1816 Clinch**. Cross 18th Street. At **1733 Clinch** on the left, you'll see an historic restoration of a large Colonial Revival called "White Columns." At the corner with 17th Street, at 1705 Clinch, you'll see the **Carson House**, a 1903 house built for W. W. Carson, a math professor at the University of Tennessee who established the chair of civil engineering there. This house has been nicely restored as the Ronald McDonald House, where parents of children in the area hospitals can stay.

At 17th Street, turn north and look for an historical marker about Fort Sanders and a stone memorial to the Confederate

Carson House

150

soldiers killed in the battle. This street actually began as a trench that was part of the fortifications of Fort Sanders.

Return to Clinch Avenue and continue east, but be careful at this crossing of 17th Street where there is no light to help you across. At **1633 Clinch** on the left, you'll find an elaborate Victorian home with rounded porch and turret built about 1889 for G. W. Pickle, an attorney general of Tennessee; the house, designed by L. C. Waters, is representative of the larger homes built toward the top of the hill on the university side of Fort Sanders. At **1625 Clinch** stands a Neoclassical home using several styles, built in 1907 but with several additions.

The 1914 house at **1604 Clinch** was the home of William Rule, founder and editor of the *Knoxville Journal* and the mayor of Knoxville in 1873 and 1898. Notice the sidelights and fanlight around the door. The house now serves as the Institute for Religion for The Church of Jesus Christ of Latter Day Saints. At the southeast corner of 16th and Clinch, you'll find a monument to the 19th New York infantry who fought in the Battle of Fort Sanders.

Turn north on 16th Street to Laurel Avenue and turn right. On the southeast corner of 16th and Laurel stands the **Laurel Theater** at 1538 Laurel, originally the Fort Sanders Presbyterian Church built in 1895-98. The theater has a variety of musical concerts.

At **1537 Laurel** on the left, you'll find an 1888 Queen Anne house designed by Joseph Baumann; the house has been modified to make apartments and may at one time have had a turret. At **1517 Laurel**, stands a typical Queen Anne with Shingle influence. Then at **1511** stands a Neoclassical Revival built in 1910 with large portico. On the right at **1502 Laurel** you'll see a house with Neoclassical influences built about 1896.

Continue on Laurel across 15th Street. The **Ross House** stands at 1415 Laurel, built with Queen Anne massing and Romanesque details in 1894. M. L. Ross was a wholesale grocer and a mayor of West Knoxville. The house has been an apartment house since the late 1930s and is now called "Laurel Terrace."

On the southeast corner of Laurel and 14th Street, notice the variety of wood moldings on the 1898 house at **1318 Laurel**. Turn right on 14th Street to Clinch Avenue and turn right, headed

151

Ross House (David Cann)

west. At the end of the block on the left at **1416 Clinch**, you'll find a Queen Anne house built in 1894 for R. T. DeArmand, a state legislator and U. S. Marshall. The house was designed by the well-known architect George F. Barber.

At 15th Street, turn left. The complex on your right is a commercial block where you'll find at the southwest corner of Clinch and 15th the **Falafel Hut**, a Middle Eastern restaurant. At White Avenue, turn left headed back east. The brick structure on the southeast corner of White and 15th was originally the carriage house for the Woodruff mansion that once stood where now the University of Tennessee's Hoskins Library stands. W. W. Woodruff was the founder in the late 1860s of Woodruff's, which still does business in the city center.

Continue east on White Avenue. The house at **1403 White** is an 1888 Queen Anne; notice the decorative trim using XO+OXO+OX. Cross 14th Street; you'll see on the northeast corner the new **UT Textiles and Nonwoven Development Center**. At **1312 White** on the right, stands an 1896 Victorian house with both Queen Anne and Shingle influences. "Judge" Charles Brown, a county chancellor, lived in the house at **1308 White**. Shingle and Queen Anne styles are both present in the house at **1302 White**, built in 1896 for C. D. Schmitt, a math professor at the university.

At 13th Street, turn left to Clinch Avenue. To the left on Clinch, at **1300 Clinch**, you'll find a Victorian home with uncommon rectangular shape. At **1310** stands a house that combines Italianate form with a round Queen Anne porch.

Turn around and head east on Clinch, passing 13th Street. The house at **1205 Clinch**, built in 1883, has been altered but still has decorative Eastlake detail. The 1876 house at **1202 Clinch** is one of the oldest houses in Fort Sanders. It was the home of Weston M. Fulton around 1900; Fulton, a UT instructor, invented the sylphon, a predecessor of the thermostat

At 12th Street, turn left to Laurel Avenue. At Laurel Avenue you can turn left to see a couple of large Queen Annes at **1213** and **1221 Laurel**, built in the late 1800s. Turn right on Laurel to return to the Arts Center on 11th Street.

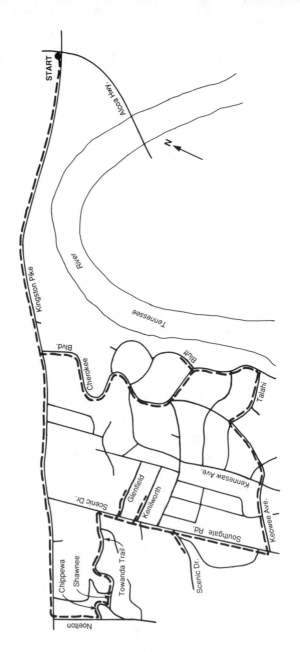

Kingston Pike and Sequoyah Hills

16 Kingston Pike and Sequoyah Hills Walk

7 miles
Connections: Lyons View and Westmoreland Heights Tour,
Bearden Tour

Attractions: This walk along Kingston Pike leads west past several historic homes and into the Sequoyah Hills area and the Talahi subdivision.

Start: Begin the Kingston Pike walk toward Sequoyah Hills west of Fort Sanders and the University of Tennessee and just west of the entrance to Tyson Park. Here, Alcoa Highway crosses over Cumberland Avenue, which at this point becomes Kingston Pike. Because of the length of this tour, you may want to walk Kingston Pike and Sequoyah Hills at separate times. The Sequoyah Hills section is ideal for bicycling.

Description: The first important road into East Tennessee was formed by settlers moving into the Holston River Valley by way of Jonesboro and Greeneville and finally to Knoxville. This road was eventually extended west of the city to Campbell's Station, later the community of Farragut. This segment between Knoxville and Campbell's Station was surveyed by Charles McClung and was the first improved road in the county. Made into a turnpike in 1866 and eventually passing to Kingston to the west, the road became known as "Kingston Pike."

Because Kingston Pike was the main road west from Knoxville, homes, some quite large, were constructed along the thoroughfare. The city's streetcar system was extended down Kingston Pike around the turn of the century. Large, elegant homes continued to be built in the area, which was annexed by the city in 1917.

Begin your walk of this neighborhood just after Alcoa Highway on the north side of Kingston Pike. You'll see on the

155

right, the **Ossoli Clubhouse** at 2511 Kingston Pike, built in 1933 by Barber & McMurry and now on the National Register of Historic Places. The Ossoli Circle that meets in the clubhouse is the oldest federated women's club in the South, founded in 1885.

Walk west from the clubhouse. You'll pass **Kingston Apartments** on the right, which provides housing for University of Tennessee married students. Next is **Tyson Junior High School**, built in 1936 by Baumann and Baumann; the building is currently unused. The school was named for Lawrence D. Tyson, a brigadier general in World War I, U.S. Senator, 1925-31, and the father of Charles McGhee Tyson for whom Tyson Park is named.

Just before reaching the end of the block, you'll see on the right **Oakwood**, a residence built in the 1870s for C. J. McClung, who then traded the house for the downtown property of his sister Lucy, Mrs. Jacob L. Thomas. The house was sold to Henry Thrasher in 1908 and extensively remodeled. Today it houses Fleenor's hair style saloon, and Josephine's, a dining club.

At the intersection with Concord Street to the right and Neyland Drive to the left, you'll be able to see among the trees to the left, on the west side of Neyland, the **University of Tennessee Faculty Club**, which was once the Eunice Miller residence, built about 1925 and later remodeled into a club with tennis courts and swimming pool. Farther south on Neyland, you can reach the Agricultural Campus of the University of Tennessee and the main campus beyond. To the north on Concord, you can find another entrance to Tyson Park.

Continue straight on Kingston Pike through this intersection. For all the time you are on Kingston Pike, you'll need to use caution, especially if children are along; Kingston Pike is still a major artery west and nearly always has heavy traffic.

You'll enter a tree-shrouded residential area containing homes built in the early 1900s interspersed with occasional historic homes built before 1900. The homes represent Mission, Spanish Colonial Revival, Victorian Romanesque, Colonial Revival, Bungalow, Neoclassical, Tudor Revival, and Queen Anne architectural styles and were designed by the well-known firms of Barber & McMurry and Baumann and Baumann, in
156

addition to lesser known architects. The historical importance of these homes, typifying suburban expansion by the upper economic class along an early transportation corridor, is the basis for proposed designation of this stretch of Kingston Pike as an historic district on the National Register.

On the south side of Kingston Pike, you'll find one of the historic homes, **Crescent Bend** at 2728 Kingston Pike, built in 1834 as a residence by Drury P. Armstrong, a merchant, farmer, and county official who probably designed his own home. The Federal-style residence is also called the "Armstrong-Lockett House" for the first and last families to use it as a residence. Today the house serves as a museum containing one of the oldest furniture collections in the Southeast, the Toms Memorial Collection of American and English furniture, and has in back the William P. Toms Memorial Gardens, elaborate terraced gardens created in 1984 that lead from the back of the house down to the Tennessee River. Toms, at one time manager of the Fulton Sylphon Company, established the Toms Foundation to manage his estate, which includes the antique furniture and silver he collected during his life.

The building with the red tile roof adjacent to Crescent Bend is the **Van Dyke Apartments** designed by R. F. Graf and built in 1927. You'll pass on the north side of Kingston Pike the **Second Presbyterian Church** and then, at 2931 Kingston Pike, the **Teen Center** located in a 1916 Italianate-style residence designed by Barber & McMurry. Teen Center, Inc., is an organization for Knoxville teenagers that trains young people for volunteer work. You'll also pass on the north **Temple Beth El**, and then at **3039 Kingston Pike** you'll see an apartment building constructed in 1928. At 3111 is **The Nicholas**, an Italianate-style apartment building constructed in the 1920s.

Across the street, you'll find the **Dulin House** at 3100 Kingston Pike, a Neoclassical residence designed by John Russell Pope, a nationally known architect, and built around 1915 as a residence for H. L. Dulin. In the recent past, this residence and the adjacent **George Taylor residence** formed the Dulin Gallery of Art, which was eventually incorporated in the Knoxville Museum of Art with a new museum building adjacent to the World's Fair Park. The Taylor residence was built in 1900 and remodeled in 1929 by Barber & McMurry. Taylor was the federal district judge for whom the University of Tennessee's George C. Taylor Law Center is named. Today the Dulin House and the Taylor residence are the sites for the singles and youth ministries of Calvary Baptist Church.

On the other side of the Taylor residence, you'll find **Bleak House**, a residence named for the Charles Dickens 1853 novel and built for Robert H. Armstrong, the son of Drury P. Armstrong who built Crescent Bend. Bleak house, built in 1858 in the Italianate style but remodeled in the 1930s, is on the National Register. The house was the headquarters of Confederate General James Longstreet during the siege of Knoxville in 1863. Longstreet stationed sharpshooters in the tower of the house. It was from here that Union General William P. Sanders was shot. In response, Bleak House was fired upon by the Union soldiers, and the house still shows the scars of bullet holes. A sketch in the tower that probably dates from the war shows three men who were shot while on guard. Today the house is a museum of period artifacts operated by the United Daughters of the Confederacy and is called "Confederate Memorial Hall" and may be toured with a small fee. Behind the house you'll find the remains of terraced gardens that were added in the early 1900s.

You'll pass **Calvary Baptist Church** on the south side of Kingston Pike, the **Tennessee Valley Unitarian Church** on the north, and then the **First United Methodist Church** on the south.

Then on the north at 3411 Kingston Pike, you'll see the **Edwin R. Lutz Residence**, built about 1927 and later remodeled. Lutz was an insurance and manufacturing executive who was the son of John Edwin Lutz and Adelia Armstrong Lutz for whom the adjacent home, **Westwood**, was built in 1890. Westwood, at 3425 Kingston Pike, is a Queen Anne house designed by Baumann and Baumann with a Richardsonian Romanesque arched stone entryway. J. E. Lutz founded the insurance business of J. E. Lutz and Co., which his son Edwin joined and which still operates in Knoxville today. Adelia Lutz was a well-known painter. The Westwood house, now on the National Register, is built on land given to J. E. and Adelia Lutz by her father, Robert H. Armstrong. The three historic houses, Crescent Bend, Bleak House, and Westwood were all part of the estate of Adelia's grandfather,

Bleak House

Drury P. Armstrong. Notice the unusual serpentine wall in front of both Westwood and the Lutz House.

Past Westwood, you'll see new residential units on the south side of the pike. Farther along, you'll come to the **Laurel Church of Christ** on the north side and, across Kingston Pike, the entrance to **Sequoyah Hills**, the first planned subdivision in Knoxville. In 1890 when there were only a few residences along Kingston Pike, the area where Sequoyah Hills is now located was proposed for an industrial site, but the plan was abandoned during the depression of the 1890s. In 1925, a North Carolina developer, E. F. Ferrel, established a company to build a subdivision on the site, which he named "Sequoyah Hills" after the Cherokee man known for having invented an eighty-six character syllabary for the Cherokee language in the early 1800s.

Ferrel continued his Indian motif by naming the main thoroughfare through the subdivision "Cherokee Boulevard." All utilities were placed underground, the roads followed the contour of the land, and trees were left whenever possible. The planned community attracted many of the upper economic class, who built large homes along Cherokee Boulevard and its side streets.

Turn left into Sequoyah Hills past the stone entrance. Although you'll usually not find sidewalks in the subdivision, traffic is almost always light and you'll not have much difficulty walking on the street. Along Cherokee Boulevard, a walking/jogging path runs down the middle of a median strip of grass and trees, which makes for a pleasant walk.

On the right at **485 Cherokee Boulevard**, you'll find a 1927 Colonial Revival brick residence designed by Barber & McMurry. Another Barber & McMurry house stands at **493 Cherokee**, a stucco built in 1927. Notice at **569 Cherokee** the large stucco Tudor Revival residence built about 1928.

At **602 Cherokee** is a Colonial Revival home built in the 1920s and designed by Ryno & Brackney, a well-known architectural firm that operated from 1921 to 1933; John H. Ryno had trained under George Barber.

A stucco Italianate-style house stands at **802 Cherokee**, built about 1927. Then at **840 Cherokee**, you'll find a 1927 Barber & McMurry house that has had recent additions. The

Tudor Revival style home at **857 Cherokee**, dating from about 1926, was one of the first homes built in Sequoyah Hills.

At the corner of Bluff Drive and Cherokee Boulevard, turn left on Bluff for a short walk to a 1930 Baumann and Baumann residence at **834 Bluff Drive** and a 1928 Barber & McMurry home, a stone Tudor Revival at **826 Bluff**.

Retrace your steps to Cherokee Boulevard and continue south. At 940 Cherokee, you'll see the **Nash House**, which is now a residence for the Chancellor of the University of Tennessee. Dr. Walter S. Nash, a surgeon, built his home in the 1890s on Main Street where the U.S. Post Office now stands. In 1930, with the post office soon to be built on the site of his home, Dr. Nash had the house dismantled and moved to this site on Cherokee Boulevard. In 1960, the house became the property of the university.

Just at the UT chancellor's home, you'll notice a concrete structure with a street light on top in the middle of the median. This marks the entrance to **Talahi**, an elaborate addition to Sequoyah Hills.

In 1926, Robert L. Foust, a developer with the Alex McMillan Company, purchased 100 acres adjoining Sequoyah Hills on the south and west to create an aesthetically planned subdivision. He called the place "Talahi," an Indian word meaning "in the oaks." This area, where Cherokee Boulevard follows along the Tennessee River as it sweeps through a large bend, was called "Looney's Bend" after Absolem Looney, who was a colonel in the War of 1812. The island in the bend of the river is called "Looney's Island." Looney died in 1859; he and the other original owners of Sequoyah Hills are buried in a cemetery on Arrowhead Trail. The cemetery, which is now completely overgrown, is marked only by an historical marker.

To add to the aesthetic appeal of his new subdivision, Foust had many park-like structures built that continued the Indian motif of Sequoyah Hills, including structures like the one you see at the beginning of Talahi. For instance, the lights at the various entrances to Talahi have near the top the figure of the water spider, which in Cherokee mythology brought fire to Earth.

Continuing south on Cherokee Boulevard, you'll come to the **Sunhouse Fountain**, which is part of a mall extending from Cherokee Boulevard into Talahi to the west. To the left, you'll see

Talahi Light (David Cann)

162

the entryway to a proposed clubhouse, which was never built. Today, this area to the left is part of **Sequoyah Park**, a mile-and-a-half-long city park that occupies the strip of land between Cherokee Boulevard and the Tennessee River.

This area of Sequoyah Hills was actually occupied by Indians at one time. To the southwest about half a mile along Cherokee Boulevard from Sunhouse Fountain, an **Indian Mound** stands in the median of the boulevard.

From Sunhouse Fountain, turn right headed west on Talahi Drive into the mall that was intended as a park for the subdivision. As was planned for Sequoyah Hills, all utilities for Talahi were placed underground, and in addition the streets were paved in concrete. The enclosed rectangle in the mall is **Papoose Park**, a play area for children. Notice the Thunderbird figures in the grillwork of the side gates. Beyond the park, you'll find **Panther Fountain**.

By the time Foust was ready to sell lots in the subdivision, he had invested huge sums of money in the development. As a result, he had to set the lot prices relatively high. Unfortunately, the lots in Sequoyah Hills were selling for a cheaper price and the other subdivision was already satisfying much of the market for high-priced housing. Only one lot was sold in Talahi, the lot for the Nash House. The company Foust formed to develop Talahi, the Mutual Development Company, had to declare bankruptcy. In 1933, apparently depressed by the failure of his great venture, Foust shot himself.

Eventually the lots in Talahi were sold and homes were constructed. Today, the subdivision is considered part of Sequoyah Hills. The Talahi improvements along Cherokee Boulevard and the streets of Iskagna, Keowee, Talahi, Tugaloo, Kenesaw, and Taliluna comprise an historic district on the National Register.

From Panther Fountain, walk northwest on Talahi Drive. Where Talahi meets Keowee Avenue, turn left. Down Keowee, you'll enter **Council Point**, a commercial district that was included in the original plans for Talahi. You'll find here shops, stores, and a bank. At the intersection with Kenesaw Avenue, keep straight on Keowee. On the right stands **Sequoyah Presbyterian Church**, designed by Baumann and Baumann, and on the left, **Sequoyah Village Apartments**. Continue west on Keowee; cross Agawela Avenue to Southgate Road. Turn right, headed north on Southgate. You'll find the **Sequoyah Branch Library** at 1140 Southgate, designed by Barber & McMurry. Continue north on Southgate to the **Sequoyah School** at 942 Southgate; Barber & McMurry also designed the elementary school, which was built in 1929.

Continue north on Southgate to Scenic Drive, and turn left for a short walk to a stone English cottage built about 1931 at **924 Scenic Drive** on your left and at **1029 Scenic Drive** on your right a 1928 brick residence designed by Barber & McMurry. Retrace your steps to the intersection, with Southgate to the right, and you'll find that Scenic bears to the left. Walk north on Scenic past Oakhurst Drive. At Kenilworth Drive, you may want to explore to the right to see the large homes there. Continue on Scenic. At **641 Scenic Drive** on the left, you'll find a Ryno & Brackney white-frame Colonial Revival residence built around 1928. Also on the left, at **631 Scenic**, stands a white-brick house built about 1929. At Glenfield Drive, you may again want to explore to the right. Then continue north on Scenic to Towanda Trail and turn left.

At **4012 Towanda**, you'll find a 1936 Barber & McMurry frame residence that has had additions made. Continue on Towanda, and then go straight on Shawnee Lane as Towanda turns right. At Chippewa Circle, turn right. At the end of Chippewa, you'll be at Noelton Drive. Turn right, and you will emerge from Sequoyah Hills on Kingston Pike. Across the pike, you'll see **Western Plaza**, the first shopping center outside of Knoxville's downtown; it has been recently renovated and little resembles the old center. Among the stores and shops are **Appletree Bookstore** and **The Half Shell** restaurant and **Ruffles & Truffles Tea Room**.

Cross Kingston Pike, and then turn right headed east to complete the Kingston Pike walk. On the north side of Kingston Pike at 4311 stands the **Montessori Children's House**, originally a residence designed by Barber & McMurry and built in 1928; the Children's House is a private school for preschool through fifth-grade children. Farther down Kingston Pike at **4243 Kingston**, you'll find a 1917 residence that is also a Barber &

McMurry design. On the south side of Kingston Pike at **4084** is a Baumann and Baumann house built in 1927. Next on the south side at 4070 stands the **St. George Greek Orthodox Church** where the annual Greek Festival is held each spring. Also on the south at **4024 Kingston Pike** is a 1913 residence designed by George Barber.

Then farther down at 3945 Kingston Pike, on the north side of the pike, is the **John Jennings Residence**, a 1926 house designed by Ryno & Brackney. Jennings was a lawyer and judge before coming to Knoxville; he practiced law here and was a U. S. Congressman from 1939 to 1951. On the south is the **Knoxville Woman's Club** at 3930 Kingston Pike; you'll find here the **Barbara Keating Gardens**.

Two houses down on the north side is the **E. H. Scharringhaus Residence**. Scharringhaus, a clothing manufacturer, was the director of the 1913 National Conservation Exhibition and apparently moved from the 4th and Gill Neighborhood when this Barber & McMurry house was built in 1926. Across the street at **3910 Kingston Pike** is another Barber & McMurry house built in 1921.

You'll pass on the north side the **Heska Amuna Synagogue**, and then at 3747 Kingston Pike, also on the north, is a Tudor Revival-style Barber & McMurry residence built in 1926 that is today **Compton Manor**, a bed and breakfast. On the south side at **3738 Kingston Pike** is a double residence designed by Barber & McMurry and built in 1925.

You'll pass the **First Seventh Day Adventist Church** on the north and the **First Church of Christ Scientist** on the south. And then on the south at **3526 Kingston Pike** you'll see another Barber & McMurry house built in 1923.

You then will have returned to the entrance to Sequoyah Hills. Behind the Laurel Church of Christ on the north side of the pike, you can connect with the **Third Creek Bicycle Trail** that parallels Kingston Pike to Tyson Park. To return to the start of the walk, continue east on Kingston Pike.

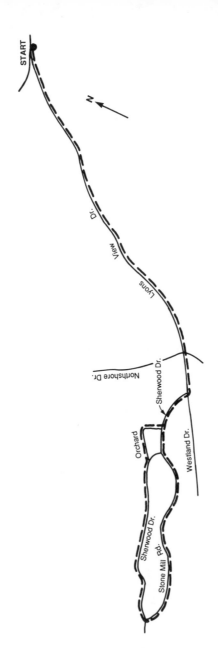

Lyons View and Westmoreland Heights

17 Lyons View and Westmoreland Heights Tour

6.5 miles
Connections: Kingston Pike and Sequoyah Hills Walk,
Bearden Tour

Attractions: You'll see many large old homes that were built along Lyons View Drive, which served as part of the corridor west from Knoxville, and one of the early city subdivisions.

Start: Because Lyons View is a very busy road with no sidewalks, this outing should be done as an auto tour. Begin at the far end of the Kingston Pike and Sequoyah Hills Walk at Western Plaza on Kingston Pike; just west of the shopping center, Lyons View Drive begins on the left. From this point, you can also keep straight on Kingston Pike to take the Bearden Tour.

Description: Lyons View is named for Capt. William Lyon who settled in the area around 1810. He purchased several hundred acres that afforded an expansive Tennessee River view that came to bear his name. At the turn of the century, the neighborhood along Lyons View Drive consisted of just a few large homes. The streetcar extended only as far as the point at which Lyons View begins on Kingston Pike. It was not until 1913 that a rubber-tired streetcar ran up Lyons View Drive.

Even then, Lyons View continued to be a residential neighborhood for the traditional upper class, closely linked in style and manor as well as geography to Kingston Pike and Sequoyah Hills. Most of the existing homes were built in the early 1900s and constitute a neighborhood that has been recommended for an historic district on the National Register. Lyons View was annexed to the city in 1917.

Begin your tour headed west on Kingston Pike from Western Plaza. Turn left on Lyons View Drive. On the right, notice the Bungalows at **4633** and **4729 Lyons View Drive**, which are here

167

J. Allen Smith House

less common than in other areas of the city. Just past Arrowhead Trail, you'll see on the left at **4734 Lyons View** a large residence remodeled in 1920 by Barber & McMurry.

In half a mile from the beginning of Lyons View Drive, you'll pass on the left a small stone church, **Mt. Pleasant Baptist Church**. Also on the left, at **5020** and **5032 Lyons View**, are two Barber & McMurry houses built in 1928 and 1919. Still on the left, at **5104 Lyons View**, is a 1925 Ryno & Brackney. Then you'll pass **Cherokee Country Club** at 5138 Lyons View, designed by Baumann and Baumann and built in 1928.

Past the country club, you'll see a 1925 residence at **5220 Lyons View** and then a 1931 Barber & McMurry house at **5308**. The 1916 Italianate-style house designed by Barber & McMurry on the right at **5305** was the house of J. Allen Smith, the founder of the company that introduced White Lily Flour. Then again on your left, you'll see several more Lyons View houses, including a 1930 residence at **5512**, and at **5522** another Barber & McMurry built in 1930.

On the right, at 0.7 mile from Mt. Pleasant Church, you'll come to the **gatehouse to Westcliff**, the later home of Weston M. Fulton. The gatehouse is now the entrance to an apartment complex that surrounds the remains of the elaborate 1928 residence based on Spanish and Italian forms that was designed by Barber & McMurry. Across from Westcliff, at **5720 Lyons View**, you'll see a large Italianate built in 1923.

In 0.2 mile from the Westcliff gatehouse, on your left at 5908 Lyons View Drive, you'll find the **Lakeshore Mental Health Institute**, originally established by the state as the Eastern State Hospital for the Insane in 1873 at the old Lyon homeplace. The original hospital building constructed in 1884 is a three-story brick Victorian Vernacular structure crowning the top of the hill within the institute grounds. You can drive in to get a closer look at the building with its parapets and Victorian porch. The structure is recommended for the National Register.

Across Lyons View Drive from the institute is the **Tennessee Veterans Cemetery**. When Lyons View runs into Northshore Drive in 0.2 mile, continue straight across on what is now Westland Drive. In another 0.2 mile, turn right into **Westmoreland Heights** on Sherwood Drive.

Westmoreland Heights Waterwheel (David Cann)

170

Around 1920, Daniel Clary Webb and his wife purchased 60 acres of farm and woodlands in what was to become Westmoreland Heights. Webb was a lawyer and the first Juvenile Court Judge in Knox County. The Webbs moved into a house already on site and pumped their water from a small spring nearby. About 1922, Ed Manning, one of the owners of the Tennessee Mill and Mine Supply Company, bought a lot from the Webbs to build a home and became the second resident. More water was needed for the emerging neighborhood, and so Manning and Webb devised a means of pumping water from a larger spring to the west by use of a waterwheel on a small creek at the entrance to the Webb estate. Manning engineered the project, and Charles Barber of Barber & McMurry designed a stone house to contain the Fitz overshot wheel. You'll see the waterwheel and stone house on the right of the entrance to Westmoreland Heights.

The water system also served the home of John J. Craig III on the other side of Westland Drive behind the new Craigland Courts just west of the entrance to Westmoreland. The 1926 Craig house was designed by Barber & McMurry. Craig was the grandson and son of the John Craig family of marble quarriers. It was under the grandson's presidency of the Craig company that the Candoro Marble plant was established on Maryville Pike and the two affiliates became a leading supplier of marble.

In 1923, a corporation was formed by Webb, Manning, and others to build the Westmoreland Heights subdivision. The homes constructed were all served by the waterwheel system. When electricity arrived, an electric pump was installed, and the waterwheel was relegated to ornamental use. The Westmoreland water system was finally connected to the city water system in 1940. The neighborhood was annexed in 1962.

On your drive, you'll see the homes of Westmoreland, most built in the early 1930s. In 0.2 mile from the entrance, turn right on Orchard. The original Webb home that stood on Orchard burned in the early 1930s; the Webbs rebuilt on Sherwood Drive. Orchard ends back at Sherwood in 0.2 mile. Turn right. Continue on Sherwood to Stone Mill Road on the left in 0.8 mile. Turn left on Stone Mill, which returns to Sherwood in 0.9 mile. Bear right on Sherwood 0.3 mile to return to Westland Drive. Return east on Westland to Lyons View Drive and back to your starting point.

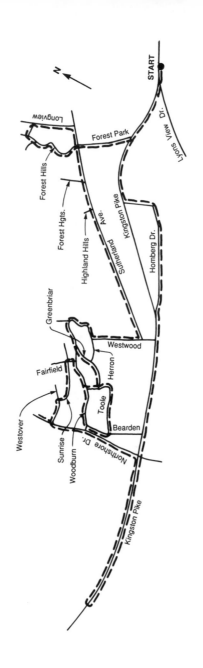

Bearden

172

18 Bearden Tour

6.5 miles
Connections: Kingston Pike and Sequoyah Hills Walk, Lyons
View and Westmoreland Tour, Third Creek Bicycle Trail,
Southwest Knox County Tour, North Knox County Tour

Attractions: This tour of Bearden goes through the
neighborhoods of Forest Hills and Westwood and by the location
of old brickyards on Homberg Drive.

Start: Because of the length involved and the stretches along
busy Kingston Pike and Northshore Drive, this outing should be
done as an auto tour. Begin at the west end of the Kingston Pike
and Sequoyah Hills Walk on Kingston Pike. Western Plaza will
be on your right. Lyons View Drive will lead off to the left for the
Lyons View and Westmoreland Heights Tour.

Description: Lyons View Drive and Westmoreland Heights are
part of what is generally called "Bearden." The community of
Bearden is loosely considered to reach as far west as Gallaher
View Road, where Bearden High School is located. Bearden
proper is the area of Knoxville west along Kingston Pike across
Northshore Drive and over the crest of Bearden Hill.

James Miller was probably the first settler in the area. He
operated a trading post until he suddenly died; two nephews were
accused of poisoning him. Jacob Lonas, a German from Pennsylvania, settled along what is now Middlebrook Pike around 1794.
John Reynolds, an Irishman who immigrated to this country,
came to Knoxville in 1817 and settled in the area of Bearden.

Reynolds named the growing community "Erin." The name
was later changed to "Cooper" to avoid confusion with another
Erin in Tennessee. Later it was called "Crippen." Finally, in
1883, the name became "Bearden," after Marcus De LaFayette
Bearden, who had a farm in the community. Bearden had been a
captain in the Union Army during the Civil War. He was twice the
Sheriff of Knox County and the Mayor of Knoxville, 1868-1869.

He also served in the state legislature and was instrumental in getting Eastern State Hospital, now the Lakeshore Mental Health Institute, located on Lyons View Drive.

The community of Bearden grew up along the western corridor created by Kingston Pike and the Southern Railway line, originally the East Tennessee, Virginia, and Georgia line. Around 1900, the community was mostly still farming country, but it had a depot on the rail line, a post office, a blacksmith shop, a grist mill, and a couple of stores. In the intervening years, many businesses have grown up along Kingston Pike while quiet neighborhoods have continued to survive on the side roads. Bearden never incorporated as a town. The community was annexed by Knoxville in portions in 1917 and 1962.

Begin the tour on Kingston Pike at Western Plaza headed west past Lyons View Drive. In 0.3 mile, turn right on Forest Park Boulevard. In another 0.2 mile, you'll reach Sutherland Avenue.

Across Sutherland is the entrance to **Forest Hills**, part of a larger neighborhood created from four developments—Forest Hills in the early 1930s, Forest Heights in the late 1930s, Highland Hills in the early 1940s, and Highland Hills Addition in the late 1940s. The combined neighborhood has since taken on the name of "Forest Heights." Cross Sutherland to Forest Hills Boulevard and enter the the oldest of the subdivisions, Forest Hills. As you travel uphill, you will be ascending Forest Heights Ridge. Once covered in pine and oak, the neighborhood still has many trees, some as much as two hundred years old. Forest Hills, which contains stone, brick, and stucco homes in primarily the Tudor Revival and Colonial Revival styles, has been recommended as an historic district for the National Register.

In 0.2 mile along Forest Hills Boulevard, you'll reach a fork with Forest Hills turning left to a deadend. Turn right on Village Road and then right again to Longview. Turn right 0.2 mile to Sutherland Avenue. To the left on Sutherland, you'll find the University of Tennessee Sutherland Apartments where at the back on the east side you can connect with the Third Creek Bicycle Trail.

Turn right on Sutherland. You'll pass through the intersection of Forest Park and Forest Hills Boulevards and in 0.1 mile the entrance to the Forest Heights section of the neighbor-

706 Forest Hills Boulevard (David Cann)

hood and in another 0.1 mile the entrance to the Highland Hills section.

You'll then pass **Highland Memorial Cemetery** on your right and then the **Bearden Post Office** on your left. Soon after, Sutherland Avenue meets Westwood Road, at half a mile from the entrance to Highland Hills. Turn right into **Westwood**, another early suburb of Knoxville. In 1925, the Knoxville Suburban Corporation acquired the land to construct a subdivision, which it called "Kingston Pike Heights." A few homes were built in the late 1920s, but with the 1930s depression, the corporation failed. In 1938, the Westwood Corporation was formed to complete the residential community.

Along Westwood, you'll pass on the left **Century Court One** and **Century Court Two**, small residential developments constructed by Stuart Fonde, a local builder. You'll reach Herron Drive in 0.2 mile along Westwood. Turn right on Herron Drive to Woodburn Drive and turn left. In 0.1 mile, bear left on Greenbriar. To stay on Greenbriar, bear right and right again and you'll rejoin Woodburn. Turn left on Woodburn to Bearden Drive in 0.1 mile, just before Northshore Drive. As you can see to the right, Bearden Drive was partially obliterated when Northshore was built. Turn left on Bearden and in 0.1 mile left again on Toole Drive. On the left in 0.1 mile, you'll find the oldest home in Westwood at **5817 Toole**, but it was moved to this location. It is believed that John Kidd Bearden, son of Marcus Bearden, built the house in 1911 in the area that became Westwood, and it was later moved to the Toole Drive location.

Stay on Toole 0.1 mile to Greenbriar; go straight and then right on Woodburn 0.1 mile to Fairfield and turn left. Very soon after, turn left again on Sunrise Drive. In 0.1 mile at 139 Sunrise, you'll find the **Reece Patterson Home**, the oldest house built for the Westwood subdivision, a Federal home constructed prior to 1928.

In another 0.1 mile you'll reach Westover Drive. Turn left 0.1 mile to Northshore Drive. Just to your right on Northshore, you can see a porcelain and steel **Lustron House** on another remaining piece of Bearden Drive at 1106, built in 1949. You'll see more Lustron houses in South Knoxville on the Southeast Knox County Tour.

Head south on Northshore Drive to Kingston Pike, 0.3 mile from Westover. Turn right on the pike and ascend Bearden Hill. In 0.3 mile, notice the large home on the right that crowns the hill. The Georgian-style house was built in 1851 for Robert B. Reynolds, the son of John Reynolds and a major in the quartermaster department during the Mexican War and later paymaster in the army. During the Civil War, General Longstreet used the house, called "**Knollwood**," as his headquarters prior to the siege of Knoxville.

At the top of Bearden Hill, find a convenient place to turn around and return to Northshore Drive. If you were to turn right on Northshore, you would soon come to Baum Drive, named for Baum's Florist that once had a farm in Bearden with many greenhouses for its florist business, originally headquartered in Fountain City.

This intersection is also the beginning of the Southwest Knox County Tour, to the south on Northshore, and the North Knox County Tour, to the north on Northshore.

Continue east on Kingston Pike, and in 0.5 mile, turn right on Homberg Drive. At the junction, you'll pass **Naples Italian Restaurant** on the right and then **The Orangery** restaurant on Homberg. In 0.2 mile on the right, you'll see **Cherokee Porcelain**, which produces porcelain products, such as signs, and has a porcelain facade similar to the Lustron houses. Homberg then parallels the railroad tracks on the right. On the left at 5103 Homberg is the **Wallace Chapel African Methodist Episcopal Church**, built in 1930. The church is a remnant of a black community that once existed along the tracks. The blacks settled in the area to work in brickyards that were located next to the railroad.

At the end of Homberg Drive in 0.2 mile at Kingston Pike, turn right 0.6 mile to return to your starting point at Western Plaza.

Knollwood (David Cann)

19 Bicentennial Park

Attractions: Bicentennial Park is the beginning of a waterfront development that will take advantage of Knoxville's location on the Tennessee River.

Directions: The park is located on the south side of Neyland Drive, across from where Walnut Street leads uphill into the city center. You can get on Neyland Drive either from Kingston Pike on the west or from the Business Loop on the east.

Description: J. G. M. Ramsey, considered by many to be Tennessee's first historian, states in his *Annals of Tennessee*, that during the negotiations for the Treaty of Holston in 1791 Gov. William Blount sat at the treaty ground at the foot of Water Street, now called "Central," and was surrounded by tall trees that shaded the bank of the Holston River, now called the "Tennessee." From this description, it is apparent that the Treaty of Holston was signed at the location where First Creek flows into the Tennessee River. In 1976, to celebrate the nation's bicentennial and to preserve this treaty ground, the City of Knoxville established **Bicentennial Park** along the riverfront were First Creek joins the Tennessee River.

Bicentennial Park is also where the Union Army erected a pontoon bridge across the river during the the the siege of Knoxville in 1863. The federals needed a supply line across the river and also needed access to Fort Dickerson on the south side of the river. The pontoon bridge was located approximately where **Gay Street Bridge** now spans the river above the park. In 1962 one of the anchors for the pontoon bridge was discovered during a dredging operation and is now on display at Confederate Memorial Hall (Bleak House) on Kingston Pike.

Rumors that the Confederates were building a raft to float down the river to break through the bridge caused the federal forces to string an iron chain upstream of the bridge to stop the raft. The Confederate raft never arrived, but the chain was used

Robert E. Lee

to catch and retrieve rafts of supplies that farmers loyal to the Union sent down the river.

Bicentennial Park is a small strip of land that runs between Neyland Drive and the Tennessee River. It's here that you can board the **Robert E. Lee Riverboat** for cruises on the river while having dinner. You'll also find a riverside restaurant, **Calhoun's**.

Long-range plans for the city call for waterfront development that includes an outdoor stage and amphitheater for riverside entertainment and a system of walkways and bicycle paths linking downtown and traveling along the river. There's even talk of uncovering First Creek, which presently runs through a culvert buried under the Business Loop. The first modest step in this waterfront development will be a **Bicentennial Walk**, projected to be completed in 1991, that will link the riverfront with James White Fort, Blount Mansion, and the city center.

At present there is a half-mile walk and bicycle path on the west end of Bicentennial Park that parallels the riverbank. Along this path, you'll find the **Municipal Boat Dock**. At the end of this walk you will be at the mouth of Second Creek. You can take a path up to Neyland Drive and continue west to connect with the University of Tennessee Campus and farther along the UT Agricultural Campus and Tyson Park. You'll also find at the end of the path that you can walk down to the boat dock and then pass upstream along Second Creek by a walkway under Neyland Drive and, by continuing north, pass through the parking area that once connected the main 1982 World's Fair Site with the amusement park that operated during the fair. You will emerge on Cumberland Avenue at the corner of 11th Street. To the left, you can begin the University of Tennessee Campus Walk; to the right, you can join the World's Fair Park Walk; and straight ahead up 11th Street, you can reach the beginning of the Fort Sanders Neighborhood Walk.

20 Chilhowee and the Knoxville Zoological Park

Attractions: Chilhowee Park is the traditional place in Knoxville for staging fairs, while the adjacent zoo is nationally known for its breeding capabilities with rare species.

Directions: From the city center, head east on Magnolia Avenue three miles to Chilhowee Park on the left. Turn up Beaman Street to get to the entrance.

Description: Each September the Tennessee Valley Fair is held at Chilhowee Park. Amidst displays of award winning vegetables, livestock, and farm machinery, you can attend art displays, music concerts, and food booths and take a ride in the amusement park. Each evening ends with a fireworks display.

Chilhowee Park has long been the site of Knoxville's fairs. The tradition began with the Appalachian Exposition of 1910, which was staged to bring regional and national recognition to Knoxville. Exhibit halls were constructed that were used to display the region's agricultural, mineral, and forestry products and the accomplishments of its people. The local marble industry constructed a large marble bandstand in the center of the exhibition area that was designed by R. F. Graf.

Visitors came from many states, and former President Theodore Roosevelt attended. The first airplane in Knox County was flown around Cal Johnson's nearby race track. The exposition was so successful, it was held again the next year, and President William Howard Taft attended. Two years later, in 1913, the National Conservation Exposition was held at Chilhowee Park to draw attention to the conservation of the natural resources of the region and the nation; conservation was a new concept at the time. Grand buildings were constructed to house the exhibits. Booker T. Washington was the guest of the exposition. The National Conservation Exposition was the last of the great expositions held in Knoxville until the World's Fair in 1982, which was held in the city center.

Chilhowee Park Bandstand (David Cann)

Before the turn of the century, Chilhowee Park was known as "Lake Ottossee," for the lake in the park. The first electric streetcar line led from the city center to Lake Ottossee. The park was owned by the Knoxville Railway and Light Company that operated the streetcar line. After 1900, an amusement park was constructed on the shore of the lake, and the name was changed to "Chilhowee."

In addition to the main expositions in the early 1900s, smaller expositions were held, such as the 1916 East Tennessee Division Fair; J. G. Sterchi, one of the founders of the Sterchi furniture chain, served as president of the 1916 fair. In 1921, Sterchi bought Chilhowee Park from the Railway and Light Company and renamed it "Sterchi Park," which he opened for the use of the people of Knoxville. In 1926, he sold the park to the city without making a profit, and the name was changed back to "Chilhowee."

Today, Chilhowee is a city park where you can picnic and walk along the lake. You'll find here the **marble bandstand** from the early fairs, the only structure remaining from the early exposition buildings; all the other original buildings burned.

You also find here the **East Tennessee Discovery Center**, a museum of natural, physical, and social sciences designed to interest school children. You'll also find at the back of Chilhowee the **Knoxville Zoological Park**, which has a national reputation for the breeding of animals. It was here that the first African elephant in the Western Hemisphere was born. The zoo can be reached on Prosser Road off Magnolia Avenue.

21 Tyson Park and the Third Creek Bicycle Trail

Attractions: Tyson Park offers outdoor recreation and anchors the eastern end of the Third Creek Bicycle Trail.

Directions: You'll find Tyson Park on the north side of Cumberland Avenue/Kingston Pike just west of the University of Tennessee Campus.

Description: As a lieutenant in the U.S. Navy Air Corps during World War I, Charles McGhee Tyson, son of Lawrence D. and Bettie McGhee Tyson, died in action over the North Sea in 1918. In 1929, Mrs. Tyson donated property for a park in an agreement with the city that Knoxville would always have an airport with the name "McGhee Tyson." McGhee Tyson Airport was first located on Sutherland Avenue, but it was soon too small to handle the air traffic. In 1935, with federal assistance and small contributions from Maryville and Alcoa, Knoxville began construction of a larger airport south of Knoxville in Blount County. Some wanted the name to be the "Great Smoky Mountains Airport." But Knoxville Mayor George Dempster remembered the obligation to Mrs. Tyson and insisted on the name "McGhee Tyson." While the Knoxville City Council approved the Tyson name, those opposing it had an act passed in the state legislature making the name "Great Smoky Mountains Airport." In the opening-day celebrations of the new airport, the McGhee Tyson name was used and in practice is still used today.

Tyson Park also bears Charles McGhee Tyson's name. The park is a favorite place for picnicking and tennis. But it is also known for being the eastern end of the two-mile **Third Creek Bicycle Trail**, which is used for both bicycling and walking.

The bicycle trail follows Third Creek upstream to the west. To follow the trail from the park's west entrance on Concord Street, cross Concord and walk or bike west on Painter Avenue. In a quarter mile, the street deadends as the paved bicycle path leads straight into the woods. For the next mile and a half, the trail wanders through a second-growth woods, occasionally crossing bridges as the trail crisscrosses Third Creek.

At about one mile along the trail, you'll reach a connector trail to the left that leads up to the back of the Laurel Church of Christ on Kingston Pike.

The trail ends at the University of Tennessee Sutherland Apartments on Sutherland Avenue. From this west end you can walk or bike out to Sutherland and turn west to connect with the Forest Hills section of the Bearden Tour.

Also from Tyson Park, a short bicycle trail to the south follows Third Creek downstream to the **University of Tennessee Agricultural Campus**. The trail begins by crossing Third Creek on a wooden bridge near the Cumberland Avenue entrance to the park. You'll find on the agricultural campus small gardens and greenhouses that constitute an **open garden** that you can browse through. On Jacob Drive, you'll also find the **Trial Garden** where annuals and perennials are grown from seeds donated by floral companies to be evaluated under East Tennessee growing conditions.

From the Trial Garden, you can also walk or bike to the junction of Jacob Drive with Neyland Drive and turn east on Neyland to reach in 1.3 miles the Thompson Boling Arena on the back of the UT Campus and, in another half mile, the beginning of the Bicentennial Park Trail on the river side of Neyland Drive.

Across the river from Neyland Drive, you'll see a steep cliff crowned by apartment buildings. From that vantage point, called "**Cherokee Heights**," Confederate General James Longstreet tried to shell Fort Sanders during the siege of Knoxville in 1863. The attempt failed because of the distance and the low-grade gunpowder that was available. This was also the location of a cable car that in the 1890s carried people to the south side of the river. The cable stretched from about where Third Creek enters the Tennessee River to the top of Cherokee Heights. The cable car ceased operation in 1894 when during a passage a cable snapped, killing one person and leaving several people stranded above the river until they could be rescued.

22 Ijams Park and Nature Center

Attractions: Wildflowers, birds, and woodland walks are the special attractions at Ijams Park.

Directions: From the city center, cross the Tennessee River on the Gay Street Bridge and turn left on Sevier Avenue. When Sevier bears to the right in 0.7 mile, continue straight on Island Home Avenue for another 0.7 mile. Straight ahead is the Island Home Park neighborhood. Keep right on Island Home Avenue; in 0.2 mile turn left to stay on Island Home. Watch for the Island Home Baptist Church on your left in another 0.6 mile. In another half mile you'll come to the entrance to Ijams Park on the left.

Description: In 1910, Harry P. Ijams and his wife, Alice Yoe, built a home on a 26-acre tract of land that was once part of the Perez Dickinson Island Home Farm. The Ijams turned their small estate into a garden showplace where such groups gathered as the Knoxville Area Audubon Society and the Girl Scouts.

As a memorial to the Ijams, the City of Knoxville in 1964, with a federal grant and the help of the Knox County Council of Garden Clubs and the Knoxville Garden Club, purchased 20 acres of the property, including the **Ijams Home**, and established **Ijams Park** (pronounced without the "j"). Since 1976 the park has been managed for the city by the **Ijams Nature Center**, a non-profit agency promoting environmental awareness.

Ijams is open to anyone wanting to get away from the bustle of the city. The **Discovery**, **Fern Walk**, and **Pine Succession Trails** wander by nature gardens, a spring-fed pond, and the bank of the Tennessee River through a second-growth woodland that is known for its bird population. In addition there's the quarter-mile paved **Serendipity Trail** for the handicapped. In 1990 an additional 63 acres were added to the park that was once part of the old Meades Quarry, an abandoned marble quarry you can see by continuing out Island Home Avenue. New trails will be constructed into this additional acreage when a master plan for use of the area has been developed.

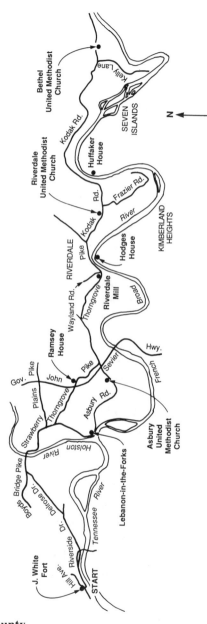

East Knox County

23 East Knox County Tour

38 miles
Connections: The Early Days Walk

Attractions: East Knox County was the site of the first settlements in the Knoxville region; the tour includes Ramsey House and the Riverdale Community.

Start: Across Hill Avenue, just west of James White's Fort at the beginning of The Early Days Walk, take Riverside Drive headed east along the Tennessee River. Distances between sites are given in mileages, so you may want to zero your odometer.

Description: At 0.7 mile, Riverside Drive turns right and passes under South Knoxville Boulevard. Just after, you'll pass the **McCammon House** on the left at 1715 Riverside. This was the home of Samuel McCammon, Knox County Sheriff in 1838-50. The house, built in 1849-50 and now on the National Register of Historic Places, is occupied by Engert Plumbing and Heating, Inc. This is also the site of James White's second home in Knoxville. After the new Knoxville settlement took on the shape of a town, White probably wanted to escape the confines of the settlement and moved to this location about a mile east of First Creek. White's home on this site, a two-story log house, was dismantled in 1852-53. A marker erected in 1901 on the southwest corner of the lot, along Laurens Street, designates the spot.

Just past the McCammon House, you'll see on the left at **1811 Riverside Drive** a two and a half-story Queen Anne home built about 1905 and recommended for the National Register. In 0.2 mile past this house look for the **Mark B. Whitaker Water Plant** on the right, one of the first water pumping stations for the city, built in 1926-27. The plant is a Gothic Revival two-story brick building that has been recommended for National Register listing. Whitaker was a general manager of the Knoxville Utilities Board.

In another 0.3 mile, you'll find another residence recommended for the National Register, the **Williams House**, at 2225 Riverside, a two-story brick Federal home built in 1842.

Continue out Riverside Drive, and in another 0.3 mile bear left on Delrose Drive as Riverside curves right. In another 1.4 miles, you'll reach Boyds Bridge Pike; turn right. You'll cross Holston Hills Road, where to the left you can join the Holston Hills section of the East Knoxville Tour. You'll then cross the Holston River. Notice straight ahead the grand, two-story frame house on the knoll overlooking the river, built about 1900. Once across the river, you will have left the Knoxville City Limits and will be on Strawberry Plains Pike in Knox County. In one mile from the bridge, bear right on Thorngrove Pike, and then in 0.2 mile bear right on Asbury Road.

The community of Asbury was settled around 1786. Asbury was a Methodist bishop who conducted the first Methodist service in Knoxville in 1800. At 2208 Asbury Road, on the left at 0.5 mile from the beginning of Asbury Road, you'll see the **Weigel House**, a large frame house with wrap-around porch built in 1908. Southwest of the house, notice the old springhouse.

In another half mile, as Asbury Road reaches the point of land at the confluence of the Holston and French Broad Rivers, you'll find on your left the site of the **Lebanon-in-the-Forks Presbyterian Church**. This was the first church in Knox County, organized in 1791 by Rev. Samuel Carrick who came to the area in 1790. Carrick later organized the First Presbyterian Church in the city center and was the president of Blount College, the forerunner of the University of Tennessee. The original stone church on this site was replaced in 1903 with a new frame building that burned in 1981. As a memorial, a pavilion has been constructed on the site using the church columns that survived the fire. Under the pavilion you'll find the old church bell. The cemetery surrounding the church site contains some of the pioneers of the area, including F. A. Ramsey, who accompanied James White on his first exploration of the region in early 1780s. Ramsey's son, J. G. M. Ramsey, is also buried here, as is Elizabeth M. Carrick, "consort of S. Carrick."

In 0.2 mile past the church site, notice the large marble quarry on your left. Quarries were operated in this region of the

190

Asbury United Methodist Church

county beginning around 1871, and a community called "Marbledale" was established east of Asbury. Although marble has long been a major industry in Knox County, the demand for marble has declined over the years. Continuing out Asbury Road, you'll cross National Drive in one mile from the quarry.

An owner of marble quarries in the area built the 1890 Victorian house with Neoclassical columns at **2721 Asbury Road** 0.1 mile past National Drive; the house has been recommended for the National Register. Notice the carriage blocks by the front gate that were once used to step up into carriages or to mount horses. In 0.3 mile past the house, you'll find the **Asbury United Methodist Church** on your left, a Gothic Revival built around 1900 in a style similar to that used in many Methodist Churches built during the period.

As you continue on Asbury, you'll cross Gov. John Sevier Highway in 0.5 mile. Soon after, Asbury joins Thorngrove Pike. As you drive out Thorngrove, you'll reach a fork at 1.3 miles from Sevier Highway where Thorngrove bears right. As you continue on Thorngrove, you will enter the community of Riverdale. It was in this region that James White first settled in 1785 before moving with his family to the site that became Knoxville. On your right at 1.4 miles from the fork on Thorngrove, you'll see the **Kennedy House**, built in 1830 by James Kennedy in the Greek Revival style. The front porch is a later addition. Kennedy was a Presbyterian minister who had immigrated from Ireland.

Just past the Kennedy House, turn left on Wayland Road. You'll see immediately on the left the **Riverdale Mill**, built around 1850 and now on the National Register. The earliest record of the mill shows that it was owned by James Kennedy, Rev. James Kennedy's son. The two-story wood-frame mill of post and beam construction sits on the tract of land that was first settled by James White. At one time there were 57 mills in Knox County that served the local citizens, primarily for grinding wheat and corn. You'll find now the remains of only a few.

The Riverdale Mill stands near the location of Bowman's Ferry. The mill and ferry probably helped in providing supplies to the Union troops in Knoxville during the 1863 siege, in which supplies were floated down the river to Knoxville. The mill passed through several owners since Kennedy. In 1908, it was

192

Riverdale Mill

modernized with the addition of roll mills and a 30-foot overshot steel Fitz wheel to replace the millstones and the wooden wheel. A long flume brought water to the top of the wheel from a dam you'll find upstream along Wayland Road. In 1953, the mill machinery was removed and the mill used for storage. The present owners have restored the Riverdale Mill, using the machinery from another mill.

The Riverdale Mill was once an integral part of the self-sustaining community of Riverdale, which had a tannery, blacksmith shop, general store, school, and church. The **one-story frame home** across from the mill with the long front porch was once the post office.

Continue east on Thorngrove Pike. In 0.2 mile from Wayland Road, you'll be at the approximate location where Bowman's Ferry crossed the river. The ferry was later called "Hodges Ferry" and then "Riverdale Ferry." Across the French Broad River, the **Hodges House** stands on a knoll. The house was built in 1836 by the operator of the ferry; a later owner added the wrap-around porch and Eastlake detailing. It is one of only three known houses in Knox County that uses a rubble fill in the walls as insulation, a technique called "noggin." The house has been recommended for the National Register.

At 0.5 mile, on the left, notice the **two-story frame house** built in the 1890s. Across the road is another **two-story frame house** built about 1840. At this latter house, notice the "spirit" door on the second floor, which was used to more easily get furniture into the second story. When a person died, these doors were opened to supposedly allow the spirit to leave. Just past these houses, you'll see the **H & H Service Mart**, a typical trade center, built about 1880; scenes in the movie *The Dollmaker* were filmed at the old store.

At 0.1 mile past the store, turn right on Kodak Road. Soon on the left, look for a **Queen Anne house**, built in the 1880s. Then in another 0.2 mile on the right is a **Victorian Vernacular house**, a two-story brick built in the late 1800s. In another 0.5 mile, you'll find the **Riverdale United Methodist Church**, built about 1890.

In 0.2 mile from the church, turn right on Frazier Road. This small country lane takes you into the **Frazier Bend Community**, originally settled around 1790. The remaining homes date from the early 1800s. Located in a bend of the French Broad River, the settlement illustrates the importance of the river system as a means of transportation in the early years of Knox County settlement. In 0.5 mile on the right in the trees, you'll see a two-story frame house using the Greek Revival style. A second two-story frame house stands on the right in another 0.1 mile. Continue for another half mile to a house dating from the early 1800s (as the road bends right keep straight up the hill). Then in another 0.4 mile, you'll swing around a one-story house also built in the early 1800s. Probably built of logs that are now covered with weatherboard, the house is one of the earliest to be built in the river community. From this house you have an expansive view of the French Broad River and its floodplain.

In this region, the French Broad makes several sweeping turns. In the early years, newcomers tended to settle on the peninsulas in these river bends. Across the river from Frazier Bend is a similar river community called "Seven Islands" that is part of the Southeast Knox County Tour. The next community up river is in a bend called "Kelly Bend."

Turn around at a convenient place and return to Kodak Road. If you want to also visit the Kelly Bend Community, turn right on Kodak. At 0.7 mile from Frazier Road, at a pulloff and boat ramp into the river, you'll be at the location of Huffaker Ferry, which operated about the same time as the Hodges Ferry. You'll see the two-story frame **Huffaker House** on the other side of the river, built in the 1850s.

Road access into Kelly Bend is very limited. But once you get around to Kelly Bend, you'll see along Kodak Road some of the early structures, and at 3.9 miles from the Huffaker Ferry site, you'll also find the **Bethel United Methodist Church**. Although relatively simple in design and architecture, the church is another of the early churches constructed in the same period as the Asbury and Riverdale churches.

If you explore Kelly Bend, retrace your route back along Kodak Road to Frazier Road. Then continue on Kodak Road back to Thorngrove Pike and then left along Thorngrove Pike back to the junction with Asbury Road at 4.5 miles from Frazier Road. But instead of turning left on Asbury Road, continue straight on

Thorngrove Pike. In 0.3 mile notice the two-story Bungalow built about 1920 with tile roof on your right at **2903 Thorngrove Pike**. Just past the house at the intersection with Cinder Lane, you'll also see a general store, also built about 1920.

Pass straight through the intersection, and on your right in another half mile, you'll find **Ramsey House**, the home of Francis Alexander Ramsey, built in 1795-97. Ramsey, along with James White, was a member of the early team of surveyors that explored the region in the early 1780s. Ramsey claimed land in the forks of the rivers and settled there in 1792 or 1793 near Swan Pond. The pond was frequented by ducks, geese, and swans, which is how it got its name. The Ramsey family first lived in a log house, during which time Ramsey had the pond filled in, either because of the mosquitoes that bred in the shallow water or to discourage the Indians who came there to fish.

Ramsey brought Thomas Hope from Charleston to build his mansion that was originally called "Swan Pond." Hope was an English architect and builder. The two-story house of red marble and blue limestone with attached kitchen was considered the finest house of its day.

James G. M. Ramsey, the son of F. A. Ramsey, became a physician and author of the state's first history, the *Annals of Tennessee*. He later built a grand mansion for himself in the Asbury Community; "Mecklenburg," as it was called, was burned during the Civil War.

Ramsey House is today a national historic site on the National Register. The home is administered by the Knoxville Chapter of the Association for the Preservation of Tennessee Antiquities and is open to the public with a fee. The house contains period furniture and antiques.

From Ramsey House, continue west on Thorngrove Pike to where you cross Gov. John Sevier Highway. Stay on Thorngrove Pike, past your original turnoff on Asbury Road, to Strawberry Plains Pike at 1.5 miles from the Ramsey House. In 1.0 mile on Strawberry Plains Pike, you'll travel back across the Holston River to Boyds Bridge Pike. In 0.4 mile from the bridge, turn left on Delrose, and then in 1.4 miles rejoin Riverside Drive, which leads back to the city center at James White's Fort.

Ramsey House

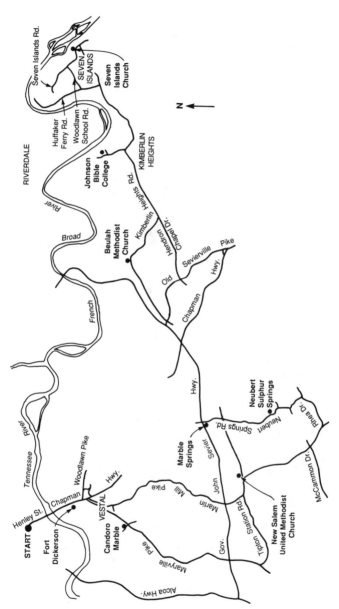

Southeast Knox County

2⁴ Southeast Knox County Tour

56 miles
Connections: Fort Dickerson

Attractions: The Southeast Knox County tour takes you by early settlements along the French Broad River and the home of John Sevier.

Start: Cross the Tennessee River on the Henley Street Bridge and head south on Chapman Highway. Mileages are given between most sites.

Description: In 0.8 mile from the Henley Street Bridge, you'll pass on your right the entrance to **Fort Dickerson**. A park was established on this site in 1936 to preserve the fortifications that remain from the Civil War. Prior to the siege of Knoxville in 1863, Union General Ambrose Burnside realized that whoever controlled the hill overlooking Knoxville on the south side of the Tennessee River could easily shell the town and drive out the occupying army. One of the primary purposes of the pontoon bridge that the Union Army constructed across the river was to be able to get troops and supplies to that strategic location. The Union Army constructed a fort of earthworks on the summit of this hill, and in fact from Fort Dickerson, Union troops were able to turn back Confederate cavalry that advanced from the south during the siege of Knoxville.

Before entering Knox County, turn left on Woodlawn Pike just past the Fort Dickerson entrance to see some architecturally distinct Knoxville houses. In 0.3 mile, at 325 Woodlawn Pike, you'll see on the left the **Graf-Cullum House**, built in 1923; the house is in the Prairie style, which is relatively unique to Knoxville. The house was designed by R. F. Graf as a residence for himself; Graf was the architect for many Knoxville buildings, including the Moses School in Mechanicsville and the Sterchi and Arcade Buildings in the city center. Across from the Graf-Cullum House, turn right on Southwood into a neighborhood of

1920-40 homes, including a number of stone houses. You'll soon reach a fork; bear right on Chamberlain and then right again. At **222 Chamberlain**, on the left, notice the unusual porcelain and steel house, another of the Lustron houses like the one in the Westwood subdivision in Bearden. These houses consist of steel joists and trusses covered with porcelain-enameled steel panels, a very durable construction, but difficult to put together. There are only a few hundred in the country.

After the Lustron house, you'll find another fork; bear left on Glenhurst Road. At **3510 Glenhurst** on the left is another of the porcelain houses. These two houses, both of which were built about 1947, are half of the Lustron houses in Knox County. In addition to these two and the one in Bearden, the only other known Lustron house is one at 1043 South Garden Road in Sequoyah Hills.

Glenhurst curves right to join Chapman Highway. Turn right on Chapman 0.1 mile to Maryville Pike on your left. Turn on Maryville Pike headed southwest. In 0.4 mile you'll join William Blount Avenue; bear right and then turn left in front of the **Mary Vestal Park** to stay on Maryville Pike. The community of Vestal was named for the Vestal family; three brothers ran the Vestal Lumber and Manufacturing Company, one of the largest lumber companies in the South. The Knoxville operations were located on Old Maryville Pike. Mary Vestal, for whom the park was named, was the family's mother.

At 0.4 mile from the park, you'll find **Candoro Marble** at 681 Maryville Pike, a building designed by Charles Barber as the headquarters of Candoro Marble Company. The marble structure was built in 1923 for the John Craig family of marble dealers and quarriers. The John J. Craig Company, which began in 1878, and its subsidiary, Candoro Marble, became the largest producer of Tennessee pink marble in the region, supplying marble for many buildings in Knoxville and other cities, including the National Gallery of Art in Washington, D. C. Candoro was a marble finishing plant, and it was here that Albert Milani worked. An Italian marble carver, Milani arrived in Knoxville in 1913 and soon became known for his carvings, which include the eagles at the top of the Knoxville Post Office in the city center. The Candoro Marble building is no longer in use.

Candoro Marble

As you continue along Maryville Pike, you'll leave the Knoxville City Limits and enter Knox County. At 1.1 miles from Candoro Marble, look for a two-story frame Victorian Vernacular at **1513 Maryville Pike** on your right that is apparently abandoned. The house and Candoro Marble have been determined to be eligible for the National Register of Historic Places.

Continue on Maryville Pike for another 2.5 miles where you'll cross under Gov. John Sevier Highway. At 0.4 mile farther, you'll see the **Maxey House** on the right, an 1830 two-story house with additions made in 1860. The house represents typical homes during the settlement of South Knox County.

In another 0.3 mile, turn left on Tipton Station Road. Notice on the left in 0.4 mile the Victorian Vernacular built about 1875 with wrap-around porch. In another 1.6 miles, you'll join Martin Mill Pike. Turn right 0.4 mile to an intersection where Tipton Station Road separates left from Martin Mill Pike. You'll bear right on Martin Mill Pike, but first turn in the driveway on the left to see the **New Salem United Methodist Church** at 2417 Tipton Station Road. The church, built in 1893 in a similar architectural style as other late-1800 Methodist churches in the county, is on the National Register. The adjacent cemetery contains the ancestors of the region's families—the Goddards, the Frenches, the Ellises, the Halls.

Continue up Martin Mill Pike. In 1.6 miles notice the two-story frame Vernacular on your left and across the road on your right the large Bungalow house. In another 0.4 mile, turn right on McCammon Road. You'll travel through rolling farm country 1.2 miles to the **McCammon House**, a large Victorian with Eastlake detailing built about 1890. In another 0.3 mile, notice the cantilever barn on your left. At a convenient place, turn around and drive back to Martin Mill Pike and turn right continuing south. In 0.6 mile from McCammon Road, you'll find a two-story frame house on the left built in 1880 in the East Tennessee Vernacular style but with Eastlake detailing.

In another 0.1 mile, turn left on Rhea Drive. In 1.0 mile you'll reach Neubert Springs Road on the left. Turn left on Neubert. At 0.4 mile bear right and in another 0.3 mile bear left to stay on Neubert Springs Road. Then in 0.8 mile farther, you'll see a gazebo on your right. This is all that is left of **Neubert Sulphur**

Springs, one of the many spas that operated in Knox County around the turn of the century. The gazebo is unique in that it is made of twisted tree roots.

Stay on Neubert Springs Road and you'll cross Tipton Station Road in another 1.2 miles. Soon after, you'll see on your left the back of **Marble Springs**, the home of Gov. John Sevier; to enter you'll have to get on Gov. John Sevier Highway. A little farther, turn right at the access road, and when you get to Sevier Highway, turn left. You'll find the entrance to Marble Springs on your left in 0.3 mile. A fee is charged to tour the Sevier homestead. Of the several period log structures in the compound, you'll find the original two-story log cabin, built in 1792, where Sevier and his family lived periodically until his death in 1815. Among the artifacts, you'll see Sevier's traveling case and cherry secretary and Catherine Sevier's brass tea kettle, banquet tables, and sideboard. The home, called "Marble Springs" because of the marble deposits and numerous springs on the property, is on the National Register.

From the John Sevier Home, head east on Gov. John Sevier Highway. At 2.1 miles, turn left to get on Chapman Highway, US441, headed south. At 3.0 miles from the turn off Sevier Highway, turn left on Valgro Road. You'll soon intersect with Old Sevierville Pike. You'll see across the road the **Valley Grove Baptist Church**. Turn left on Old Sevierville Pike. In 0.2 mile, you'll see on the left an 1850 two-story frame house in the **Greek Revival** style.

Continue up Old Sevierville Pike, bearing left; in 1.2 miles from the Greek Revival house, turn right on Hendron Chapel Drive. In another 1.7 miles, you'll join Kimberlin Heights Road.

In 1.4 miles along Kimberlin Heights, you'll see the **Gap Creek Christian Church** on your right as you enter the Kimberlin Heights Community, started in 1786 originally as Greene's Station. This was another of the river communities that depended on the French Broad for transportation. The community was later called "Manifold's Station" and then "Gap Creek" before finally it was named "Kimberlin Heights" after Jacob Kimberlin, an early settler. In 1887, a great-grandson of Kimberlin, Dr. Ashley S. Johnson, established a correspondence Bible college at the old Kimberlin homestead. In 1893, he opened **Johnson Bible**

Gov. John Sevier's Marble Springs

College for the training of Christian Church ministers; the college still operates today.

At half a mile beyond the Gap Creek Church, turn left to get to the entrance to the college grounds. Most of the buildings on the campus were constructed in the early 1900s. Probably the oldest building is the two-story frame house that serves as the president's home, which is to your right on the circular drive on the school grounds. At the northeast corner of the campus, stands the first school building, erected in 1893; notice all the stained glass. To the right is the **Irwin Library**, built in 1912. The Johnson Bible College Campus has been recommended as an historic district for the National Register.

From the college turnoff, continue east on Kimberlin Heights Road, bearing left. At 1.4 miles, 1.9 miles, and at 2.4 miles from the college, you'll see the **Trundle Houses**. All three were built in 1910 in the Neoclassical Revival style by a carpenter, Lee Massey, for three brothers of the Trundle family. The houses have been recommended for the National Register.

At 0.1 mile past the third Trundle House, you'll find on your left the **Ridgeway Baptist Church**, built about 1900. Continue straight on Kimberlin Heights Road 0.8 mile to its junction with Seven Islands Road. Turn left to enter the **Seven Islands Community**, an early settlement in a bend of the river at a point where there are seven islands in the French Broad. You'll pass the **Seven Islands Missionary Baptist Church** on your left, and then at 0.2 mile after your turn, you'll reach on your right the **Seven Islands Church**, built about 1880. It was a Methodist Church when it was organized in 1803. The present building appears to be no longer used.

In 0.6 mile from the church, turn left on Woodlawn School Road. In another 0.6 mile, you'll find the **Keener-Hunt House** on the left just before Woodlawn School meets Huffaker Ferry Road. Along with the two-story brick Federal built in the 1830s, notice the servants' quarters, smokehouse, and other outbuildings. Keener was a widow who settled here with her seven children in the early 1800s.

Right on Huffaker Ferry Road is a deadend, but if you head that way 1.1 miles you'll find the **Huffaker House**, a two-story frame house built in the 1850s that was the home of Justus

Huffaker, one of the earliest settlers in the region and operator of a ferry across the river. This house can be seen from the other side of the river on the East Knox County Tour as you drive east from Frazier Bend toward Kelly Bend.

At a convenient place, turn around and drive back on Huffaker Ferry Road, which in 1.7 miles from the Huffaker House connects with Kimberlin Heights Road at the second Trundle House. Turn right on Kimberlin Heights. In 3.8 miles, bear right to stay on Kimberlin Heights Road when Hendron Chapel continues straight. In 1.6 miles, you'll see the **Beulah United Methodist Church** on your right. Built in 1892-94, the church is another of the old Methodist churches built in a similar Gothic design. This church is nearly identical to the New Salem Church on Tipton Station Road.

Continue on Kimberlin Heights Road 1.6 miles to where you will connect with Old Sevierville Pike. Turn right and then left to reach Gov. John Sevier Highway once again.

To complete the Southeast Knox County Tour, turn left on Gov. John Sevier Highway. You can reach Alcoa Highway in about seven miles and then turn right to head back toward Knoxville. But for a more interesting drive and to return to your starting point, turn right on Martin Mill Pike about five miles along John Sevier Highway. In 3.4 miles on Martin Mill, you'll reenter the community of Vestal at the intersection of Martin Mill and Ogle Avenue. Look to the left on Ogle to see the **Vestal United Methodist Church**, a Gothic Revival built about 1925. Just past Ogle, you'll see the **Knoxville Chiropractic Center** on your right in a house originally built about 1920 as the residence of Pierce Pease, who ran a dental laboratory for a time on Clinch Avenue in the city center.

At 0.7 mile from the intersection with Ogle, you'll reach Chapman Highway. Turn left one mile to recross Henley Bridge to the city center.

Beulah United Methodist Church

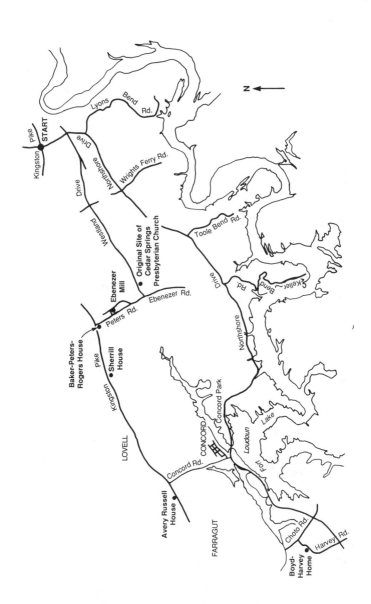

Southwest Knox County

208

25 Southwest Knox County Tour

35 miles
Connections: Bearden Tour, Lyons View and Westmoreland
Heights Tour, North Knox County Tour

Attractions: Southwest Knox County experienced similar early
river settlement patterns as East and Southeast Knox County. But
in addition, this region of the county saw development along the
western transportation corridor anchored by Kingston Pike.

Start: This driving tour begins at the intersection of Kingston
Pike and Northshore Drive on the Bearden Tour. You can also
connect with the North Knox County Tour north from this
intersection. The mileage is given for the distances between sites.

Description: At the intersection of Kingston Pike and
Northshore Drive, head south on Northshore Drive. In 0.7 mile,
you'll intersect the Lyons View and Westmoreland Heights
Tour, with Lyons View Drive to the left and Westland Drive to
the right. Turn right on Westland. You'll soon pass the entrance
to Westmoreland Heights on the right.

Continue on Westland; bear right 0.7 mile from Northshore
as Nubbin Ridge Road takes off to the left. In another 1.2 miles,
you'll cross Morrell Road and enter Knox County. In 1.1 miles,
at **8204 Westland** on the left, you'll see a Victorian cottage, built
about 1910. Then in another 0.8 mile, notice on the left at **8508**
and **8528 Westland** Victorian homes built about 1890 and 1850.
These houses represent settlement along the western corridor
created by Westland Drive and the railroad, which is on your
right.

In another half mile, you'll reach the original site of the
Cedar Springs Presbyterian Church at the New Covenant
Baptist Church. A drive on your left leads up to the churchyard
and cemetery. The continuation of the drive from the churchyard
is a private driveway that leads to **Glenmary**, also called
"Maplegrove," built in 1825 or earlier. Unfortunately you cannot

Glenmary

see the the two-story brick Federal residence with Georgian-style influences. The importance, though, is that this was the site of the home of Samuel Graham Ramsey, a Presbyterian minister who settled there in 1796. In addition to founding the forerunners of Cedar Springs Presbyterian Church, which is now located on Kingston Pike, Ramsey established Ebenezer Academy on this plantation, a school attended by his nephew, J. G. M. Ramsey.

The Ebenezer Community was named for Ebenezer Byram, who settled in the area about 1786 near Ten Mile Creek. The creek crosses Kingston Pike about ten miles west of Knoxville.

Get back on Westland from the church site and continue on Westland for 0.3 mile to where Westland meets Ebenezer Road. Turn right. In 0.1 mile, notice the **Victorian home** on the left, built about 1880. You'll then cross the railroad tracks and come to a junction where Ebenezer bears to the right and Peters Road leads to the left. Turn left on Peters Road. In 0.4 mile at the top of the hill, you'll find **Statesview**, the home of Charles McClung, the surveyor who laid out the streets and lots that became the City of Knoxville in 1791. McClung was also the surveyor for the original route of Kingston Pike. The house was built in 1804 and was given the name "Statesview" because it afforded a view of a large part of the state, from the Smokies on the east to the Cumberland Plateau on the west. The house was designed and built by Thomas Hope. The house burned in 1824 but was rebuilt. When McClung died in 1835, the house was purchased by Frederick S. Heiskell, who with his brother-in-law founded the Knoxville *Register*, a weekly newspaper that ran for 47 years. Heiskell called the house "Fruit Hill," for all the fruit trees he planted. The house is now on the National Register.

Continue on Peters Road 0.1 mile to the bottom of the hill with George Williams Drive on the right. Turn right on Williams Drive 0.1 mile until it meets Ebenezer Road. You'll see to the right **Ebenezer Mill**, constructed in 1870 on Ten Mile Creek; the mill is on the National Register. The **Atchley House**, constructed in 1905, was the miller's house. You'll see the house on the left just past the mill on Ebenezer Road.

Turn around at the mill and return on George Williams Drive to Peters Road and turn right. In a half mile you'll reach Kingston Pike and, on your left, the **Baker-Peters-Rogers House**, built about 1840 as the home of Dr. James Harvey Baker, who was killed during the Civil War by Union soldiers as he cared for wounded Confederates in his home. The house was purchased by the George Peters family in the late-1800s, and in the early 1900s the house became the home of V. M. Rogers. A monument on the grounds, keeps alive the memory of Dr. Baker's son, Abner, who died in 1865, "a martyr to manliness and personal rights." Abner Baker, a Confederate soldier who had returned home after the war, got in a fight with William Hall who was a Unionist. Hall reportedly started it by hitting Baker with a stick. Baker killed Hall in the ensuing fight and was imprisoned. In the night a group of soldiers took Baker from the jail and hanged him.

You'll also notice on the corner with the house a new gas station. In 1989, plans for the station called for demolishing the Baker-Peters-Rogers House, which caused a public outcry and much media coverage. The public involvement resulted in the gas company keeping the house intact and selling it to a dentist who intends to make an office complex of the house. **Abner's Attic Restaurant** is now open for lunch on the second floor.

Turn left and head west on Kingston Pike. You'll see along the pike that the farmland of what was also known as "Grassy Valley" has been converted to commercial development with small offices and shopping centers. As Knoxville's young middle class continues to push westward, businesses have followed.

At 9320 Kingston Pike, 0.7 mile from Peters Road, stands the **Sherrill House** on the left, a Federal brick home built about 1840. The house was originally the home of the Walker family, early settlers in Ebenezer.

As you continue along Kingston Pike you'll pass through the community of Lovell, or "Loveville" as it was first called when settled by Robertus Love in 1797 or 1798. With its tannery, store, blacksmith shop, and cobbler's shop, it was once an important community on the way west from Knoxville.

At 3.9 miles from the Sherrill House, you'll find the **Matt Russell House**, on the right, built about 1840. The house sits behind the Taco Bell and is currently unused. The two-story brick Federal home is also typical of early settlement along Kingston Pike. In another 0.4 mile, at 11409 Kingston Pike, stands the **Avery Russell House**, a two-story brick Federal home on the

212

Matt Russell House

National Register built about 1835.

An early fort settlement stood near the site of the Avery Russell House. In 1787, David C. Campbell, a colonel in the Revolutionary War, built the fort west of Knoxville that became known as "Campbell's Station." The next year, a road was opened west across the Cumberland Plateau to the Cumberland River settlements. Campbell's Station became an important trading post. In 1792, the newly formed Knox County authorized the building of a road from Knoxville to Campbell's Station, which became Kingston Pike. In 1824, Campbell sold his station to Samuel Martin, who opened a race track there. He also built an inn that later became the Avery Russell House; Russell was a merchant in the community. It was at Campbell's Station during the Civil War that the Confederates put up an unsuccessful last-minute fight to keep Union General Burnside out of Knoxville.

The community that grew up around Campbell Station is now known as "Farragut," for David Glasgow Farragut who was born in the area and during the Civil War distinguished himself as a Union Commander in the naval battles at New Orleans and Mobile Bay. It was at Mobile Bay that Farragut reportedly said, "Damn the torpedoes. Full speed ahead." He was the country's first admiral, a rank created to honor him.

Campbell Station, later Farragut, which recently incorporated, lost its prominence as a trading center with the coming of the East Tennessee and Georgia Railroad in 1853. The rail line by-passed the station by two miles to the south. A new town, Concord, was laid off along the rail line in 1854 and soon became the center of the community. By 1887, it was the largest community in the county outside of Knoxville. In 1944, much of Concord was covered by Fort Loudoun Lake when Fort Loudoun Dam was built downstream on the Tennessee River.

Turn around at a convenient place after the Avery Russell House, and in half a mile back east from the house, turn right on Concord Road. In 0.1 mile, notice the **large barn** on the right, built about 1925. In another 0.3 mile you'll pass on the right the **Pleasant Forest Cemetery** where the second governor of Tennessee, Archibald Roane, is buried. Roane lived nearby in the community. He was elected governor in 1801 when John Sevier could not run again because he had already served three consecu-

214

tive terms. Roane ran for reelection for the following term, but was defeated by Sevier, who was once again eligible to run after having skipped a term.

In about 0.2 mile past the cemetery, notice the **stone house** on the left. The house was built about 1930 by the Winfrey brothers, local stonemasons who through depression-era federal projects worked on several federal buildings in Washington D. C. Then on the right, you'll catch a glimpse of the **Hackney Mill**, a grist mill built about 1890. The mill is set down from the road on Turkey Creek. Just past the mill, notice the two-story **East Tennessee Vernacular farmhouse** that was likely the miller's house, built about 1888.

In another 0.9 mile, you'll see **Callaway's Landing** on the right. This large home with surrounding buildings constructed around 1909 on the Turkey Creek embayment of the river was a landing for river traffic. Across from Callaway's Landing, turn left on Lake Ridge Drive to enter **Concord**. The small village with its buildings constructed 1850 to 1930 has been recommended as an historic district for the National Register. In the 1880s, marble was a big business in Concord. Surrounding the town were marble quarries, and a marble polishing mill was erected in 1883. The marble was shipped on the train that ran through the community. When Fort Loudoun Lake was created, it rose to cover part of the town and all of the marble quarries.

Along Lake Ridge Drive, on your left, you'll see a couple of Victorian cottages constructed 1890-1920. The brick home at **11017 Lake Ridge** was built about 1840.

In 0.3 mile from the beginning of Lake Ridge Drive, you'll enter a commercial district constructed about 1900. You'll see on your left an old stone grocery store and then the old post office and a bank. Just past the bank building, stands the **Crichton Memorial Baptist Church**, built in 1926 and now the Calvary Evangelical Church.

You can tour the neighborhood of Concord by turning left off Lake Ridge and wandering along the streets lined with Victorian style houses. Don't miss the boarded up **Masonic Lodge** on 2nd Street, back in the direction of Concord Road. The brick Victorian building constructed about 1867 was in the 1940s and 1950s a movie theater. Back on Lake Ridge Drive, return to

Concord Bank and Post Office

Concord Road. Turn left 0.1 mile to Northshore Drive.

To see additional old homes typical of early river settlement, turn right on Northshore. In 1.3 miles, on the left, you'll pass the **Concord RV Campground**. In another 1.4 miles, you'll cross Choto Road. Then in 0.8 mile, turn right on Harvey Road.

In 0.1 mile on the right, you'll see a large frame house built about 1894 for Henry Harvey. In another 0.4 mile, on the left, you'll see another large house built in the early 1900s. Then in 0.4 mile, you'll see a large brick Federal on the left, the **Boyd-Harvey Home**, that is listed on National Register. The house was built for Baxter Boyd about 1837. In 0.1 mile, Harvey Road intersects with Choto Road. Turn right to return to Northshore in 0.7 mile, and turn left to head back to Concord. On the left in 0.2 mile at the **Montvue Farm**, notice the large Victorian house in the distance. In 2.5 miles you'll be back at Concord Road. Keep straight on Northshore Drive headed east.

In 0.8 mile, you'll pass the entrance to **Concord Park**, which was developed along the shore of the lake after it formed. In another 2.2 miles is the **Carl Cowan Park**, and then in 0.4 mile, the **Admiral Farragut Park** on your right.

Southwest Knox County experienced similar early settlement along the Tennessee River as did East Knox County along the French Broad. You'll see a few old houses on Northshore and pass roads that lead into bends in the river where early settlement took place—Keller Bend, Toole Bend, and Lyons Bend.

In 1.5 miles east on Northshore from Farragut Park, watch on the left for a large **barn and silo** with decorative brick patterns, built about 1920 and later converted to a home. On the right stands a **two-story brick house**, built about 1840.

In 3.7 miles, you'll pass Morrell Road to the left and Wrights Ferry Road to the right. In another 0.7 mile, watch for the two-story Victorian house on the left built around 1890 at **7103 Northshore Drive** and then in another 0.1 mile a Victorian cottage on the left also built about 1890 at **7003 Northshore**. In another 1.3 miles you'll reach the junction with Lyons View Drive to the right and Westland to the left. You can turn right on Lyons View to head back toward the city center or continue straight to reach your starting point at Kingston Pike.

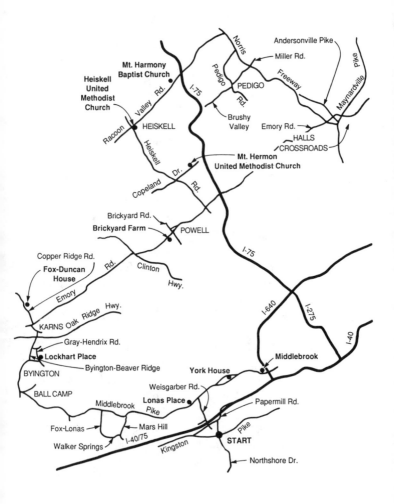

North Knox County

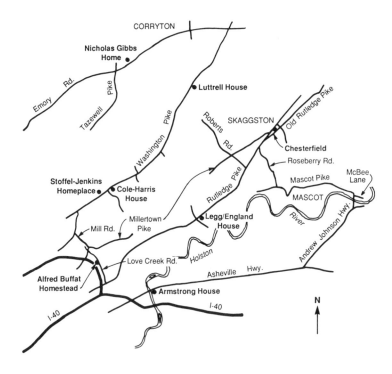

CORRYTON

Nicholas Gibbs
Home •

Emory Rd.

Tazewell Pike

Washington Pike

• Luttrell House

Roberts Rd.

SKAGGSTON

Old Rutledge Pike

• Chesterfield

Roseberry Rd.

McBee Lane

Mascot Pike

Stoffel-Jenkins
Homeplace • • Cole-Harris
House

Rutledge Pike

MASCOT

River

Andrew Johnson Hwy.

Millertown
Pike

Mill Rd.

• Legg/England
House

Holston

Love Creek Rd.

Alfred Buffat
Homestead

Asheville   Hwy.

• Armstrong House

I-40

I-40

N

26 North Knox County Tour

107 miles
Connections: Bearden Tour, Southwest Knox County Tour

Attractions: You'll pass through several early settlements and communities as you travel the main corridors of Middlebrook Pike, Emory Road, Washington Pike, and Rutledge Pike.

Start: Start where Northshore Drive crosses Kingston Pike in Bearden. This is also the beginning of the Southwest Knox County Tour. This longest outing in your exploration of Knoxville and Knox County can be divided into Northwest and Northeast Knox County Tours where the tour crosses I-75 north of Knoxville.

Description: Head north on Northshore Drive from Kingston Pike half a mile to Paper Mill Road. The road was named for the paper mill operated in the area in the 1800s by Marcus D. Bearden, for whom the community of Bearden was named, and his cousin, Gideon M. Hazen. Turn left on Paper Mill and then in 0.3 mile turn right on Weisgarber Road.

You'll cross under I-40/75. You can take a side trip left on Nightingale Lane 0.1 mile to see the **Hugh Sanford, Jr. House** built in 1923, which is now the clubhouse for the Londontown Apartments. You'll see the large house to the rear of the apartment complex.

In 0.9 mile from Nightingale on Weisgarber, you'll reach Middlebrook Pike. The tour goes left, but you can make an additional excursion to the right to see **Middlebrook**, the home of Gideon M. Hazen in 2.4 miles on the left. Middlebrook Pike was so named because it led to the house, which is located at 4100 Middlebrook Pike. Built in 1845, Middlebrook is now on the National Register of Historic Places. After you turn around and head back, watch for the **York House** in 1.1 miles at 4810 Middlebrook Pike on the left where the lanes of Middlebrook

Pike are separated by a median. The two-story brick was built in 1840.

From Weisgarber Road, head west on Middlebrook Pike. On the right in 0.4 mile, you'll see the **Jacob Lonas Place** at 6341 Middlebrook, a two-story home with wrap-around porch built about 1830 of handmade brick. Jacob Lonas was one of the first to settle in what became the Bearden area of Knoxville.

At 2.4 miles from the Lonas Place, turn left on Mars Hill Road, which marks Knoxville's City Limits. In 0.2 mile at **645 Mars Hill** on the right, you'll see a two-story brick house built about 1845. Continue on Mars Hill another half mile to Walker Springs Road. Turn right. You'll pass through a residential community 0.9 mile to the junction of Walker Springs with Fox-Lonas Road; continue straight on Fox-Lonas, which joins Middlebrook Pike in another 0.6 mile. Turn left to continue northwest on Middlebrook Pike.

In 0.7 mile on the left, you'll see **Smoky Mountain Farm Steakhouse and Beef Market**, where you can get hamburgers and steaks. At 0.4 mile farther along Middlebrook, you will enter the community of **Ball Camp**, named for Nicholas Ball, a Revolutionary War veteran who received a land grant in the area, where he established a camp. He was killed by Indians in 1793 as he and others were delivering a load of corn to the blockhouse at Well's Station, 20 miles away. Ball Camp eventually became a small community with one store, a tanyard, a church, and an academy. Germans and Pennsylvania Deutsch were among those that settled in the area. Ball Camp has remained a farming community that is centered around the **Ball Camp School**, which you'll see to your right at the junction with Ball Camp Pike 1.9 miles after entering the community.

Continue straight on Middlebrook Pike from Ball Camp Pike. In 0.1 mile, bear right at a junction with Lovell Road to the left. Bear right again at a junction in another 0.1 mile with Hardin Valley Drive to the left. In 0.9 mile you'll go through a narrow railroad underpass. Then turn right on the Byington-Beaver Ridge Road as you enter the community of **Byington**. In 0.1 mile, turn right on the Byington-Solway Road. In 0.4 mile turn left on Gray-Hendrix Road. You'll see on the right the **Lockhart Place**, a 1927 East Tennessee Vernacular construction that encloses a 1798 log house at 2516 Gray-Hendrix Road. The house with its old stone fence has been recommended for the National Register.

In another 0.3 mile you'll come to a junction with Garrison Road. Turn left 0.2 mile to get back to the Byington-Beaver Ridge Road. Just to your left on Byington-Beaver Ridge, you may want to backtrack to see on the left a lovely **Victorian house** built in the late 1800s with a bay window on the porch.

North on Byington-Beaver Ridge Road in 0.4 mile, you'll cross Oak Ridge Highway, which leads left to Oak Ridge in Anderson County. This is the **Karns** Community. After crossing Oak Ridge Highway, bear left on Beaver Ridge Road. In another 0.3 mile, you'll reach Emory Road.

Emory Road has long served as a route westward. In 1779, Evan Shelby, one of the first to settle in the Bristol area, began an expedition with 600 volunteers against the Chickamaugas, a splinter group from the Cherokees who objected to the treaties that gave Cherokee land to the whites. The Chickamaugas led by Dragging Canoe had continued to raid throughout the East Tennessee area in spite of the treaties. Shelby's force gathered in upper East Tennessee and floated down the Holston and Tennessee Rivers to the Chickamauga towns near Chattanooga. They destroyed the towns, but the Chickamaugas survived and continued their resistance until peace was negotiated in 1794.

After their raid on the Chickamauga towns, Shelby and his men returned to their homes by land, along the way blazing a trail from the Emory River to the Holston. This route eventually became an important corridor to the west and remains today as Emory Road, which stretches through North Knox County.

Turn right on Emory Road. In 0.1 mile, turn left on Copper Ridge Road. At the corner stands an old **Methodist Church/ Masonic Hall**, a brick Victorian building constructed in the 1860s that has served as a church and then as a Masonic Temple and now appears unused. A half mile up Copper Ridge Road you'll find the **Fox/Duncan House** at 3800 Copper Ridge on the right. Called "Hillbrook," the Federal brick house with Victorian porch was built in the 1830s for Reuben Fox whose slaves made the bricks. Notice also the springhouse nearby.

Fox-Duncan House

At a convenient place, turn around and return to Emory Road. Turn left to continue northeast on Emory. Because Emory Road served as an early route to the west, some of the earliest houses were built along the road. Watch for several homes built in the late 1800s, two-story frame houses and cottages with Victorian, Gothic, and Eastlake influences. At 4.2 miles from Copper Ridge Road, you'll reach Clinton Highway. Turn right and in 0.1 mile, turn left to continue on Emory Road into the community of **Powell**.

In half a mile from Clinton Highway, notice the cross-style English barn on the hill to the left that is the old **Broadacres Dairy Barn**. Broadacres Dairy was started in 1931 by Walter Weigel, whose ancestors had settled in the forks of the French Broad and Holston Rivers after arriving from Hamburg, Germany, in 1847. In 1958, Broadacres became Weigel's, Inc., which operates Weigel's Jug o' Milk Farm Stores throughout Knox County.

John Manifee was the first settler in the Powell area. He claimed land granted to him for service in the Revolutionary War. He built a cabin there in 1787 that was known as "Manifee's Station." The Bells were perhaps the second family to settle in the area. The community grew, and in 1860 a line of the East Tennessee, Virginia, and Georgia Railroad was built through the town. The depot was named for Columbus Powell, a prominent resident, and the town has been known as "Powell" since then.

Columbus Powell lived in a brick house, a two-story Federal built about 1850 with later additions at 0.5 mile from Weigel's on the right side of Emory Road. The brick for the house had been handpressed, and the home was called "**Brickyard Farm**." Powell's daughter Lillie married J. Allen Smith, who came to Knoxville in 1873 and in 1881 established a grain business that included a flour mill. J. Allen Smith and Company became known for its White Lily flour, named for Lillie Powell. The White Lily Foods Company Plant still operates under new owners in Knoxville's city center.

The railroad through Powell contributed to the community's growth. Along the rail line, businesses grew up that included shipping cordwood to Knoxville and a brickyard that turned out brick for about 40 years beginning in 1889. The community of

Brickyard Farm

Powell with its late-Victorian architecture has been recommended as an historic district for the National Register.

At half a mile from Brickyard Farm, turn right on Brickyard Road where you'll find the **Brown Homeplace** in 0.3 mile. The house with barn and smokehouse was built in the mid-1800s. Hardie Brown was one of the first settlers in the area. The community's first school was located here, and part of the Brown house was used to board students.

At a convenient place, turn around and return to Emory Road. Cross Emory on Brickyard Road. You'll cross the railroad tracks, and then at the next corner, turn right on Spring Drive. The street takes you through the old residential section of Victorian frame houses and cottages built in the early 1900s. Continue on Spring Drive until you rejoin Emory Road. At the junction notice the two-story frame house on the right.

Bear left to continue on Emory Road; notice the Gothic cottage on a side road to the left. In 1.1 miles, turn left on Heiskell Road. In 0.7 mile stands a **home with Italianate detailing**—brackets, window trim, consoles supporting door entablature. In another 0.7 mile, turn right on Copeland Drive half a mile to **Mt. Herman United Methodist Church**, established in 1894; the building was constructed around 1897. Turn around at the church and return to Heiskell Road and turn right.

In 2.5 miles, you'll reach Racoon Valley Road in the community of Heiskell. Just before the junction stands the **Heiskell United Methodist Church** on the right, another late-1890s church building. Turn right on Racoon Valley. In 1.4 miles, watch on the left for the **Mount Harmony Baptist Church**, a third late-1890s church.

In a mile farther on Racoon Valley Road, you'll cross over I-75. If you've had enough for the day, you can turn south to Knoxville. If you want to continue, head straight on Racoon Valley Road. In 1.9 miles, look on the right for a **Carpenter Gothic one-story frame house** with smokehouse, corn crib, barn, and springhouse. The farmplace, constructed 1885-1895 and now apparently unused, is an example of an early self-sufficient farm.

In another 0.2 mile, you'll reach the Norris Freeway that leads left to the historic community of Norris in Anderson

County. Turn right on the freeway a half mile to Pedigo Road on the right. In 1.4 miles along Pedigo Road you'll cross the junction of Miller Road to the left and, just beyond, Brushy Valley Road to the right and enter the community of **Pedigo**. In 0.1 mile farther, look for a Victorian Vernacular cottage on the left and just past it a two-story frame mill constructed in the 1800s. These structures, representative of early settlement and the mill industry, have been recommended for the National Register.

At a convenient place, turn around and return along Pedigo to Miller Road and turn right. In 0.9 mile, you'll return to the Norris Freeway. Turn right. In 3.5 miles, you'll enter the community of **Halls Crossroads** and reconnect with Emory Road. Turn left. In 0.3 mile you'll pass through the junction of Emory Road with Andersonville Pike, which leads northwest to Andersonville in Anderson County. It was because of the intersection of these two early thoroughfares that a community grew in the area. It was originally settled by Thomas Hall on a Revolutionary War land grant in 1796; his grandson, Pulaski Hall, established a general store at the crossroads using money he made in the California gold fields in the 1860s. Halls Crossroads has since grown into a heavy commercial area in the direction of Knoxville.

From the juncture of Emory Road with Andersonville Pike, continue 0.3 mile to Maynardville Pike, which leads north to Maynardville in Union County. South, the highway passes over Black Oak Ridge into Fountain City were it becomes Broadway. Continue on Emory Road across Maynardville Pike. On your right you'll find what remains of the **Halls Elementary School**. Built in the early 1900s with later additions, the two-story brick schoolhouse was one of the first consolidated schools in the county. Long used for storage after it had lost its usefulness as a school, the building burned in 1990.

In 2.8 miles, watch for the **Shipe Homeplace** on the right, a two-story frame Victorian Vernacular built about 1900 that was the home of the Shipe family. In another 2.0 miles you'll reach Tazewell Pike. Cross the pike, still on Emory Road, and in half a mile look for the **Nicholas Gibbs Home**, a one and a half-story hewn-log house built in 1793 that was the home of one of the county's earliest settlers and for whom the Gibbs Community is

227

named. The home, now on the National Register, is set back from the road on the left.

Continue on Emory Road. In 2.8 miles from the Gibbs Home, you'll cross railroad tracks and enter the community of **Corryton**, first settled by Col. John Sawyers, a Revolutionary War soldier, in 1785. He built a two-story log house and surrounded it with a stockade. At first the place was simply known as Sawyer's Station, but as a community grew up around the fort, it was called "Floyd." In 1887, the Knoxville, Cumberland Gap, and Louisville Railroad was built through the community, and much of the land around the station was purchased by Corryton M. Woodbury, who hoped to establish a town that he named for himself. Corryton never grew much beyond a farming community.

As you continue on Emory Road, you'll cross Corryton Road at 1.4 miles from the railroad tracks and, in another 1.4 miles, pass the site of Sawyer's Station, marked by an historical marker on the right. In 0.9 mile farther, you'll reach the junction with TN61 to the left and Washington Pike to the right. Turn right on Washington Pike.

In 1.0 mile, bear right to stay on Washington Pike. In another 0.1 mile, notice the large **Victorian cottage** on the left and then in another 0.2 mile a two-story frame Victorian Vernacular house on the left built about 1810 known as the **McBee-Sawyer-Harris Home**. These two homes are representative of early settlement in north Knox County.

As you travel along Washington Pike, you'll notice **House Mountain** to the left, the highest point in Knox County. The State of Tennessee recently acquired the mountain for a State Natural Area and will soon provide access and hiking trails.

In 3.3 miles from the McBee Home stands a two-story **Victorian Vernacular** house on the right. In another 0.3 mile, at 8300 Washington Pike on the left, sits the **Luttrell House**, a 1908 one and a half-story Victorian with Eastlake detailing.

In 4.5 miles from the Luttrell House, watch for the **Cole-Harris House** on the left at the corner of Harris Road and Washington Pike, a two-story brick built about 1800; the later owner, Simon Harris, was a Revolutionary War veteran.

Then in 0.1 mile on the right, watch for the **Stoffel/Jenkins Homeplace**, a two and a half-story Queen Anne with wrap-around porch built about 1904. The Stoffel Home represents Swiss settlement in this portion of northeast Knox County. Many of the French Swiss that immigrated to Knox County in the 1800s settled along Washington Pike. In 0.7 mile from the Stoffel Home, notice the two-story **Victorian Vernacular** on the right. And then in another 0.8 mile, you'll get a glimpse of the **Babeley House**, another Queen Anne with wrap-around porch built in 1902, also representative of Swiss settlement. The house is set back from the road to your left.

In 0.2 mile from the Babeley House, past Babeley Road, turn left on Mill Road. In 0.7 mile, you'll reach Millertown Pike; turn right. In 0.1 mile turn left on Love Creek Road. In 0.7 mile on the right at 1717 Love Creek Road stands the **Alfred Buffat Homestead**. Buffat was eight years old when he arrived from Switzerland with his family in 1848. The Buffats established a farm on Millertown Pike and in 1861 erected a grist mill on Big Creek on their property. Alfred became the operator of the mill, which was known as the "Spring Place" mill. In 1867 he built the Buffat Homestead for his wife, Eliza. The house was known as "The Maples" and is today listed on the National Register. Beside the house you'll see the miller's cabin.

In 0.4 mile beyond the homestead, you'll reach **Spring Place Park** on the left where the Buffat mill was located. The Buffat mill supplied ground corn and wheat to much of Knoxville and northeast Knox County.

In 0.2 mile from the park, Love Creek Road passes under a railroad overpass and joins Rutledge Pike. Turn left, headed northeast. In 4.1 miles on the right, just past Ellistown Road, you'll find the **Arminda Store**, built about 1900, and just past the store, the **Legg/England House**, built in the 1830s as a stage-coach inn. Tennessee's James K. Polk spent the night at the house in 1845 on the way to his presidential inauguration in Washington, D. C.

In 2.4 miles from the Legg/England House, you'll reach Roberts Road to the left. Turn left into the community of **Skaggston**, named for the Skaggs family who were early settlers in the community. In 0.6 mile, you'll reach Millertown Pike and on the other side the **New Antioch Missionary Baptist Church**. Turn right on Millertown Pike. In 0.1 mile notice the cottage on the left with Gothic influences, built about 1910. In another 1.0 mile, you'll see on the left a Victorian home and then a second Victorian with Eastlake detailing. These two homes built about 1900 and recommended for the National Register are representative of early settlement in the Skaggston Community.

Just past these homes, look for **Hopewell United Methodist Church**, organized in 1826. You'll then rejoin Rutledge Pike. Turn left. In 0.7 mile turn right on Mine Road. In another 0.1 mile at Old Rutledge Pike, turn right 0.1 mile to see **Chesterfield**, built by Dr. G. W. Arnold before the Civil War; the home is in the Georgian style of architecture and is on the National Register.

At the end of Old Rutledge Pike in 0.6 mile from Chesterfield, you'll be back on Rutledge Pike headed southwest. In 0.2 mile turn left on Roseberry Road. The road parallels Roseberry Creek on the right. The creek and road were named for William Roseberry, who received one of the earliest land grants in the area.

In 1.5 miles, you'll arrive at Mascot Pike in **Mascot**. The community is a mining town that grew up in the early 1900s. The first known settler was John Erwin who bought land there in 1796. The community that developed was at first called "Meek." But few liked the name, and when the East Tennessee, Virginia, and Georgia Railroad was built through the community, the name was changed to "Mascot." Zinc was discovered in the 1850s and some surface mining occurred. About 1906 the Holston Zinc Company opened the first zinc mine in Mascot, and zinc mining became the principal activity. The American Zinc Company acquired the mines in 1910 and during their years of operation, Mascot became a company town. In 1971, ASARCO purchased the mines from American Zinc and still operates in the area.

Turn left on Mascot Pike. On your right is the entrance to the old mine complex that includes Mine #2 and the Mascot Mill. These old mine buildings and the Mascot community have been recommended for an historic district on the National Register. On the left across from the mine is Staff Road. Along the loop formed by the road are many large cottages built around 1915 that were

McBee Bridge

houses for the upper echelons of the mine staff. Continuing on Mascot Pike for 0.4 mile, you'll cross Flat Creek; notice how the creek was channelized with concrete to prevent water from leaking into the #2 Mine. No longer used, the mine is now flooded.

You'll then pass under a railroad overpass and just after, you'll pass a large frame house on the right and then several workers cottages, including a section of houses on the left with pyramidal hipped roofs.

In 0.2 mile beyond these houses, you'll cross the railroad tracks and turn right to stay on Mascot Pike. On your left will be the **Mascot Industrial Park**. In 1.7 miles, you'll pass the road on the left to ASARCO's Immel Mine. In another 0.1 mile, you'll pass under another railroad overpass and find McBee Lane on the left. At the end of the half-mile deadend road stands the **McBee House**. This 1880 Colonial Revival with gambrel roof was the home of G. C. McBee, a large landowner who operated a ferry across the Holston River. Continue on Mascot Pike, crossing the Holston River over the **McBee Bridge**, built in 1930 with three open-spandrel concrete arch spans and five deck girder approach spans. From the bridge you can catch a glimpse of the McBee House to your left. In 0.2 mile after the bridge, you'll reach Andrew Johnson Highway, which is also US11E; turn right, headed southwest.

In 2.6 miles, Andrew Johnson Highway joins Asheville Highway headed to Knoxville. At the junction, you'll find **Helma's Restaurant**, which has a country-cooking buffet. Bear right, and in 5.0 miles at 1660 Asheville Highway, on the left just before the bridge across the Holston River, watch for the **Armstrong House**, a two-story brick Federal built about 1850.

After crossing the Holston River and traveling 0.5 mile, you'll reach I-40, which you can take six miles back to the city center and then another five miles to the Paper Mill Road Exit, which will return you to Northshore Drive. If you are going to Northshore, you can take I-640 around the city center.

Surrounding Areas

Many areas surrounding the City of Knoxville and Knox County offer opportunities for walking and for touring the historic East Tennessee region.

Oak Ridge

In the 1942, a secret government installation was established just 25 miles northwest from Knoxville. Called "Site X," the installation was part of the Manhattan Project to develop nuclear weapons for use in World War II. The job at Site X, which came to be known as "Oak Ridge," was to enrich uranium for use in the atomic bombs that would inaugurate the nuclear age. After the war, the security gates and fences that surrounded Oak Ridge were removed, and in 1955 the government sold most of the installation's land to the Oak Ridgers who formed the community.

Today, Oak Ridge is an active city focused on technical research. The U. S. government continues work at three plants that are operated by Martin Marietta Energy Systems, Inc. One of the plants, called "Oak Ridge National Laboratory," has developed a worldwide reputation in energy research and development. In 1992, Oak Ridge will be celebrating its 50th anniversary.

To get to Oak Ridge, take I-40/75 west from the Knoxville city center for about ten miles. Turn right on Pellissippi Parkway for six miles to the small community of Solway. After crossing the Clinch River, keep straight and you'll join Bethel Valley Road. As you follow the signs to Oak Ridge, you'll bear right on Kerr Hollow Road, which becomes Illinois Avenue once you are in the city. Keep straight on Illinois to Tulane Avenue. Turn right and you'll find the **Oak Ridge Visitor Center** where you can get information and directions.

On your visit to Oak Ridge, you can see an historic graphite reactor at **Oak Ridge National Laboratory** on Bethel Valley Road and the **Oak Ridge Gaseous Diffusion Plant** on TN58 where uranium was enriched for use in nuclear power plants until 1985. Adjacent to the visitor center, you'll find the **American Museum of Science and Energy**. You'll probably also want to take a walk at the **University of Tennessee Arboretum** on Kerr Hollow Road. And there is the **North Ridge Trail**, a national and state recreation trail that runs for 7.5 miles through the northern greenbelt of the city.

Norris Community and Norris Dam State Park

The first Tennessee Valley Authority dam was Norris Dam, located on the Clinch River about 20 miles north of Knoxville. When the Norris Dam project was begun in 1933, a small town was built adjacent to the site to house the engineers, architects, and workers who would erect the dam. When the dam was completed in 1936, the town became a residential community. Today, Norris is an incorporated city listed on the National Register of Historic Places.

To get to Norris, take I-75 north from Knoxville about 17 miles to the Clinton/Norris exit. Turn right on TN61. You'll pass on the left the **Museum of Appalachia**, a nationally known collection of buildings and artifacts that is open to the public for a fee and that each October holds a "Tennessee Fall Homecoming," a festival of mountain crafts and music.

Past the museum, you'll reach US441, at this point called the "Norris Freeway." From this junction, you can cross US441 to enter the **City of Norris** or you can turn left on US441 to get to **Norris Dam**.

Along the way to the dam, you'll pass the **Lenoir Museum**, another collection of Appalachian artifacts that is open to the public with no admission fee. At the dam, you'll find the old section of **Norris Dam State Park** (615/4267461), which has cabins and a campground and where you can get lunch or dinner at the **Tea Room**. The new section of the park is a couple of miles west of the dam on US441; it has tennis courts and a swimming pool as well as cabins and a campground.

In the City of Norris, you'll find quaint Norris homes constructed in a few basic designs that were given variation by the use of different exteriors of brick, board, stone, cinder block, and
234

Norris Dam

shingles. Norris is a walking community; you'll see many local residents on the streets as you tour the town. In addition, hiking trails cross the TVA land along the river near the dam, such as the **Song Bird** and **Bluff Trails**. There are also many trails in the **Norris Watershed**, a greenbelt around the northern half of the town.

Great Smoky Mountains National Park

The U.S. Congress authorized the creation of the **Great Smoky Mountains National Park** in 1926. The City of Knoxville voted $100,000 toward the purchase of the first land for the park. With additional money raised from the State of Tennessee and the State of North Carolina and donated by John D. Rockefeller, Jr., more lands were purchased and the federal government established the national park in 1934. President Franklin D. Roosevelt attended the dedication in 1940.

The Great Smoky Mountains is today the most visited national park in the country. It encompasses over a half million acres of forested mountains draped in tumbling streams with occasional pockets of virgin woods. Hundreds of miles of hiking trails lead past waterfalls to mountain vistas unparalleled in the Southeast. Because of the diverse habitat and multitude of plant and animal species, the park is designated an International Biosphere Reserve.

To get to the national park, which is about 40 miles southeast of Knoxville, take Henley Street south across the Tennessee River where it becomes Chapman Highway, named for David Chapman who was instrumental in getting the national park established. The highway leads to Sevierville, and then US441 takes you to Pigeon Forge and Gatlinburg at the foot of the Smokies. You'll find the **Sugarlands Visitor Center** on US441 south of Gatlinburg. Perhaps a quicker route is to take I-40 east to the Sevierville exit, where you travel south on TN66 until you pick up US441 in Sevierville. You can get to a more secluded section of the park by taking Alcoa Highway out of the city, south past McGhee Tyson Airport and through Alcoa to Maryville. There you can take US321 to Townsend, which serves as the gateway to the western end of the park.

Black Bear in the Great Smoky Mountains

There are numerous campgrounds in the park and camping in the backcountry. You'll also find accommodations in the surrounding resort communities. For more information, contact the GSMNP, Gatlinburg, TN 37738 (615/436-1262).

Big South Fork National River and Recreation Area

A 120,000-acre preserve of river canyons, waterfalls, sandstone arches, and caves, the Big South Fork National River and Recreation Area is one of the newest parks in the country. The recreation area was authorized in 1974, but land is still being acquired and only recently have trails and visitor facilities been completed to make the park lands accessible.

The recreation area lies approximately 70 miles northeast from Knoxville. Travel I-75 north to the Huntsville-Oneida exit and then take TN63 west through Huntsville to US27. Turn north to Oneida where you pick up TN297 west into the park. After crossing the Big South Fork at Leatherwood Ford, you'll find the visitor center at **Bandy Creek** on the west side of the river.

People from across the country come to the Big South Fork to ride horses, bicycle, hunt, fish, paddle the river, and hike. The park's 170 miles of trails meander through a land once hunted by the Cherokee and Shawnee.

Camping is permitted nearly everywhere in the backcountry. In addition, Bandy Creek Campground next to the visitor center has 150 sites, and Blue Heron Campground near the historic **Blue Heron Mining Community** in the Kentucky section has 45 sites. You can take a train ride to the mining community on the **Big South Fork Scenic Railway** out of Stearns, Ky. (800/462-5664).

History buffs can spend an afternoon at nearby **Historic Rugby**, the last English colony in the Americas, founded in the 1880s by English-author Thomas Hughes and now on the National Register of Historic Places. You can stay at Rugby's Newbury Lodge and Pioneer House (615/628-2441). In addition, you can find accommodations at **Charit Creek Lodge** in the Big South Fork backcountry, accessible only by foot or horseback (615/430-hike). **Pickett State Rustic Park** has a campground and cabins (615/879-5821).

The Big South Fork

For more information, contact the BSFNRRA, P.O. Drawer 630, Oneida, TN 37841, 615/879-4890.

The South Cumberland

The Cumberland Plateau is a section of the Appalachian Plateau that runs through Tennessee approximately 35 miles west of Knoxville. The southern part of this plateau contains canyonlands and secluded waterfalls preserved in Tennessee state parks and state natural areas.

To get to the South Cumberland, head west on I-40. The interstate climbs the eastern slope of the plateau to an elevation about a thousand feet above the surrounding valley. Continue west to the Crossville exit and take TN127 south.

South of Crossville, you'll pass through the historic **Cumberland Homesteads**, a New Deal community built during the '30s Depression using the local Crab Orchard sandstone. **Cumberland Mountain State Park** in the midst of the community was once the Homesteads park. You can rent cabins or stay in the campground while you hike the trails along Byrd Lake and Byrd Creek (615/484-6138).

Continuing south on TN127 from the Cumberland Homesteads, you'll drop into **Sequatchie Valley**. At Pikeville, you can turn west on TN30 to get to **Fall Creek Falls State Park** with an inn, cabins, campgrounds, golf course, and tennis courts (615/881-3297). Several hiking trails lead into the park's canyons, and you'll find here 256-foot-high Fall Creek Falls, the tallest waterfall in the eastern U.S.

Farther south on TN127, you can turn west on TN8 to get to **Savage Gulf State Natural Area**, the premier wilderness area on the Plateau. Many hiking and backpacking trails wander through the canyons of this natural area.

Savage Gulf is part of the **South Cumberland Recreation Area** (615/924-2980). The SCRA consists of eight areas scattered over a 100-square-mile region that include many hiking trails to historic and geologic sites. To get to the visitor center, keep on TN127 south to Dunlap, and then pickup TN28 to continue down Sequatchie Valley. At Jasper, you'll find US41 headed north to Tracy City and the SCRA Visitor Center beyond.

Virgin Falls on the South Cumberland

Selected References

Bennett, Ann K. 1990. "National Register of Historic Places Registration for Park City Historic District." Knoxville-Knox County Metropolitan Planning Commission.

Creekmore, Betsey B. 1988. *Knox County Tennessee, A History in Pictures*. Norfolk: The Donning Company Publishers.

Creekmore, Betsey B. 1984. *Knoxville—Our Fair City*. Knoxville: The Greater Knoxville Chamber of Commerce.

Creekmore, Betsey B. No date. *Historic Gay Street*. City of Knoxville and Greater Knoxville Chamber of Commerce.

Deaderick, Lucile, ed. 1976. *Heart of the Valley, A History of Knoxville, Tennessee*. Knoxville: East Tennessee Historical Society.

Fletcher, Robert J. 1969. "An Historical Perspective of Talahi: Knoxville's First Planned Subdivision Development," Planning 4100, University of Tennessee, Knoxville.

Gaines, Danny. 1977. "Kenyon Avenue (Scott-Armstrong Block)." Architecture 4170, The University of Tennessee, Knoxville.

Giesler, Mary J. 1962. "Westmoreland Heights." Knoxville: Westmoreland Garden Club.

Hicks, Nannie Lee. 1968. *The John Adair Section of Knox County, Tennessee*. Knoxville: Nannie Lee Hicks and the Nocturne Garden Club.

"A History of the Forest Heights Neighborhood." 1986. Knoxville.

Kaplan, Susan. 1977. "Scott Avenue (Harvey/Glenwood Block)." Architecture 4170, The University of Tennessee, Knoxville.

Knoxville Heritage Committee of the Junior League of Knoxville. 1976. *Knoxville, Fifty Landmarks*. Knoxville.

Knoxville Heritage, Inc. 1981. "Historic Fort Sanders, A Walking Tour of the Neighborhood." Knoxville.

Knoxville Heritage, Inc. No date. "Kingston Pike-Lyons View Heritage Tour." Knoxville.

Knoxville Heritage, Inc. No date. "Sequoyah Style, A Self-Guided Tour of Sequoyah Hills." Knoxville.

Knoxville Heritage, Inc. No date. "A Walking Tour of Mechan-
    icsville and Knoxville College Historic Districts." Knoxville.

Knoxville/Knox County Metropolitan Planning Commission.
    1990. *A Look at Knoxville's Beginnings, Downtown His-
    toric Tour*. Knoxville.

Knoxville/Knox County Metropolitan Planning Commission.
    1990. *Life Along the French Broad River, East & South
    Knox County*. Knoxville.

Knoxville/Knox County Metropolitan Planning Commission.
    1987. *The Future of Our Past, Historic Sites Survey and
    Cultural Resources Plan for Knoxville and Knox County,
    Tennessee*. Knoxville.

Lamon, Lester C. 1981. *Blacks in Tennessee, 1791-1970*.
    Knoxville: University of Tennessee Press.

Luther, Edward T. 1977. *Our Restless Earth, The Geologic
    Regions of Tennessee*. Knoxville: University of Tennessee
    Press.

MacArthur, William J., Jr. 1982. *Knoxville: Crossroads of the
    New South*. Tulsa: Continental Heritage Press.

McDonald, Michael J., and William Bruce Wheeler. 1983.
    *Knoxville, Tennessee, Continuity and Change in an Appala-
    chian City*. Knoxville: University of Tennessee Press.

Montgomery, J. R.; S. J. Folmsbee; and L. S. Greene. 1984. *To
    Foster Knowledge, A History of the University of Tennessee,
    1794-1970*. Knoxville: The University of Tennessee Press.

O'Steen, Neal. Unpublished paper. "Extensive Research on
    UTK Buildings." The University of Tennessee, Knoxville.

Residents of Old North Knoxville. No Date. "Old North
    Knoxville Walk-About," Knoxville.

Rothrock, Mary U., ed. 1946. *The French Broad-Holston Coun-
    try*. Knoxville: East Tennessee Historical Society.

Stokely, Jim, and Jeff D. Johnson, eds. 1981. *An Encyclopedia of
    East Tennessee*. Oak Ridge: Children's Museum of Oak
    Ridge.

Strange, Richard, and Bob Whetsel. 1984. "Fourth and Gill
    Historic District Nomination to National Register of His-
    toric Places." 4th and Gill Neighborhood Organization.

Westwood Homeowners Association. 1986. "A History of
    Westwood." Knoxville.

Museums, Open Houses, and Cultural Centers

(contact for hours and admission fees)

American Museum of Science and Energy, 300 S. Tulane Avenue, Oak Ridge, TN 37830, 615/576-3200

Beck Cultural Exchange Center, Inc., 1927 Dandridge Avenue, Knoxville, TN 37915, 615/524-8461

Blount Mansion, 200 W. Hill Avenue, P.O. Box 1703, Knoxville, TN 37901, 615/525-2375

Confederate Memorial Hall (Bleak House), 3148 Kingston Pike, Knoxville, TN 37919, 615/522-2371

Crescent Bend, 2728 Kingston Pike, Knoxville, TN 37919, 615/637-3163

East Tennessee Discovery Center, 516 Beaman Street, Chilhowee Park, Knoxville, TN 37914, 615/637-1121

East Tennessee Historical Center, 314 W. Clinch Avenue, Knoxville, TN 37902-2203, 615/544-5744

Frank H. McClung Museum, University of Tennessee, Knoxville, TN, 37996, 615/974-2144

James White's Fort, 205 E. Hill Avenue, Knoxville, TN 37915, 615/525-6514

John Sevier Farm Home, 1220 West Governor John Sevier Highway, Knoxville, TN 37920, 615/573-5508

Knoxville Convention & Visitors Bureau, 500 Henley Street, P.O. Box 15012, Knoxville, TN 37901, 615/523-7263

The Knoxville Museum of Art, 410 Tenth Street, Knoxville, TN 37916, 615/525-6101

Knoxville Zoological Park, Inc., 3333 Woodbine Avenue, Knoxville, TN 37914, 615/637-5331

Museum of Appalachia, P.O. Box 359, Norris, TN 37828, 615/494-76580

Ramsey House, Thorngrove Pike, Knoxville, TN 37914, 615/546-0745

Will G. and Helen H. Lenoir Museum, Norris Dam State Park, Rt. 1, Box 500, Lake City, TN 37769, 615/494-9688

Theaters and Performing Companies

(contact for schedules)

Bijou Theater, 803 S. Gay Street, Knoxville, TN 37902, 615/522-0832

Carousel Theater, University of Tennessee, Knoxville, TN 37996, 615/974-5161

The City Ballet, P.O. Box 2506, Knoxville, TN 37901, 615/544-0495

Civic Coliseum and Auditorium, 500 E. Church Avenue, Knoxville, TN 37915, 615/544-5388

Clarence Brown Theater, University of Tennessee, Knoxville, TN 37996, 615/974-5161

Ella Guru's, 727 W. Jackson Avenue, Knoxville, TN 37902, 615/971-4287

Laurel Theater, 1538 Laurel Avenue, Knoxville, TN 37916, 615/522-5851

Knoxville Opera Company, P.O. Box 16, Knoxville, TN 37901, 615/523-8712

Knoxville Symphony, 708 S. Gay Street, Knoxville, TN 37902, 615/523-1178

Tennessee Theater, 604 S. Gay Street, Knoxville, TN 37902, 615/525-1840

Theatre Central, 141 S. Gay Street, Knoxville, TN 37902, 615/546-3926

Theatre Knoxville, 220 Carrick Street, Knoxville, TN 37921, 615/523-9862

University of Tennessee Musical Arts Series, UT Music Hall, Knoxville, TN 37996, 615/974-3241

Restaurants

(The restaurants in this list are ones on the walks and tours in this book; many others operate in Knoxville; inclusion in this list or mention in the text does not necessarily represent a recommendation; exclusion does not indicate inadequate service.)

Abner's Attic, 9000 Kingston Pike, 539-2211, L only, closed Sat., sandwiches, fruit plates, homemade desserts

Amigo's, 116 S. Central Avenue, 546-9505, L & D, closed Sun., "A Touch of Mexico"

The Bistro at the Bijou, 807 S. Gay Street, 544-0537, L & early D, closed Sat. & Sun., American cuisine

The Blakely Cafe, 5 Market Square, 522-8089, L (M-F) & D (T-Sat.), closed Sun., new American with Italian flavor

The Butcher Shop, 801 W. Jackson Avenue, 637-0204, D only, steak, seafood, and spirits

Calhoun's on the River, 400 Neyland Drive, 544-0349, L & D, beef, chicken, seafood, "Best ribs in America"

Chesapeake's, 500 Henley Street, 673-0600, L & D, Sat. dinner only, closed Sun., fresh fish and seafood

Copper Cellar, 1807 Cumberland Avenue, 522-4300, L & D, beef and seafood, sandwiches and salads

Ella Guru's, 727 W. Jackson Avenue, 971-4287, D on performance nights, international cuisine

Falafel Hut, 601 15th Street, 522-4963, B, L, & D, Middle Eastern food

The Half Shell Restaurant, 4429 Kingston Pike, 588-6431, L & D, D only Sat. & Sun., "The House of Beef and Seafood"

Harold's Kosher Style Food Center, 131 S. Gay Street, 523-5315, kosher food deli

Helma's Restaurant, 8606 Asheville Highway, B, L, & D, country cooking buffet style

Josephine's, 2633 Kingston Pike, 524-3430, L (T-Sat.), D (W-Sat.), Sun. brunch, continental food

Litton's Market and Restaurant, 2803 Essary Drive, 688-0429, L & D, closed Sun., beef, seafood, chicken, bakery products

L&N Seafood Grill, 401 Henley Street, 971-4850, L & D, mesquite-grilled seafood, chicken, steak

Lucille's, 106 N. Central, 546-3742, D only, closed Mon., American cuisine with New Orleans atmosphere

The Lunch Box, 800 S. Gay Street, 525-7421, L only, closed Sat. & Sun., soups, salads, sandwiches, desserts

Manhattan's, 101 S. Central Street, 525-4463, L & D, Sun. dinner only, all-American grill, sandwiches, salads, bar

Naples Italian Restaurant, 5500 Kingston Pike, 584-5033, L & D, D only on Sat. & Sun., Italian food

Old College Inn, 2204 Cumberland Avenue, 523-4597, L & D, mettwurst & beans, gourmet burgers, chicken, steak

131 Central Deli & Sidewalk Cafe, 131 S. Central Street, 523-4131, L & D, closed Sun., specialty sandwiches, soup, salads

The Orangery, 5412 Kingston Pike, 588-2964, L & D, D only Sat., closed Sun., American cuisine with French flavor

Patrick Sullivan's Saloon, 100 N. Central, 522-4511, L & D, closed Sun., American food, bar

Perry's, 306 & 308 Wall Avenue, 637-4455, L only, closed Sat. & Sun., soup, sandwiches, ethnic and vegetable specialties

Regas Restaurant, 318 N. Gay Street, 637-9805, L&D, D only Sat., closed Sun., American cuisine, Gathering Place lounge

Robert E. Lee Riverboat, 300 Neyland Drive, 522-4630, 1-800-522-0603, American and international food

Ruby Tuesday at the L&N, 401 Henley Street, 971-4700, L & D, salad bar, American food, bar,

Ruffles & Truffles Tea Room, 4433 Kingston Pike, 588-0439, B & L, closed Sun., salads, soups, sandwiches

Sam & Andy's Diner, 1801 W. Cumberland Avenue, L & D, 524-9505, deli sandwiches, pasta, seafood, and more

Smoky Mountain Farm Steakhouse & Beef Market, Summerwood & Middlebrook Pike, L & D, steakhouse

The Soup Kitchen, 1 Market Square, 546-4212, L only, closed Sat. & Sun., soup, homemade bread, salads, and desserts

The Tea Room, E. Park Road, Norris Dam State Park, 494-8810, American cuisine

Up Town Cafe & Bakery, 4 Market Square, 971-6878, B & L, bakery specialities, sandwiches, fruit and vegetable plates

Lodging

(The hotels in this list are ones on the walks and tours in this book; many others operate in Knoxville; inclusion in this list or mention in the text does not necessarily represent a recommendation; exclusion does not indicate inadequate service.)

The Blakely Hotel, 407 Union Avenue, Knoxville, TN 37902, 615/523-6500, luxury

Compton Manor, 3747 Kingston Pike, Knoxville, TN 37919, 615/523-1204, "Luxury at reasonable prices," includes breakfast

Downtown Hilton, 501 W. Church, Knoxville, TN 37902, 615/523-2300, moderate

Holiday Inn World's Fair at Convention Center Downtown, 525 Henley Street, Knoxville, TN 37902, 615/522-2800, moderate to luxury

Hyatt Regency, 500 Hill Avenue, Knoxville, TN 37915, 615/637-1234, luxury

The Middleton, 800 W. Hill Avenue, Knoxville, TN 37902, 615/524-8100, moderate to luxury

Radisson Hotel, 401 E. Summit Hill Drive, Knoxville, TN 37902 615/522-2600, Reservations: 1-800/333-3333, luxury

Other Books from Laurel Place

The Best of the Big South Fork
(2nd Edition)

A hiker's guide to trails and attractions of Big South Fork
National River and Recreation Area in Tennessee and Kentucky.
$6.95

The South Cumberland and Fall Creek Falls

A hiker's guide to the South Cumberland Recreation Area and
Fall Creek Falls State Park in Tennessee. $6.95

The Best of the Great Smoky Mountains
(available 1991)

A hiker's guide to trails and attractions of the Great Smoky
Mountains National Park of Tennessee and North Carolina.
$7.95

Order Form

Send check or money order to:

Laurel Place
P.O. Box 3001
Norris, TN 37828

Telephone
615/494-8121

Title	Price	Quantity	Total
The Best of the BSF, 2nd Ed.	$6.95		
The South Cum. and FCF	$6.95		
The Best of the GSM	$7.95		
Historic Knoxville	$8.95		

Subtotal	
Tenn. residents add 7.75% sales tax	
Shipping and handling*	
Total enclosed	

*Add $1.15 for shipping/handling if ordering one book or for each book
if separate mailing is requested. We pay for shipping/handling if more
than one book is ordered and mailed in one shipment to the same address.

Ship to _____

Address _____

_____

Items offered subject to availability. Prices subject to change without notice.